FOR THE LOVE OF DOG

FOR THE LOVE OF DOG

HOW DOGS THINK and the UNBREAKABLE BOND THAT CONNECTS US

Maggie Marton

A REGALO PRESS BOOK
ISBN: 979-8-88845-691-0
ISBN (eBook): 979-8-88845-692-7

For the Love of Dog:
How Dogs Think and the Unbreakable Bond That Connects Us

Cover Design by Conroy Accord
Cover photography by Austyn, Carmel, Indiana

Publishing Team:
Founder and Publisher – Gretchen Young
Editorial Assistant – Caitlyn Limbaugh
Managing Editor – Aleigha Koss
Production Manager – Kate Harris
Production Editor – Rachel Paul

As part of the mission of Regalo Press, a donation is being made to IndyHumane, as chosen by the author. Find out more about this organization at: https://indyhumane.org/

This book, as well as any other Regalo Press publications, may be purchased in bulk quantities at a special discounted rate. Contact orders@regalopress.com for more information.

This is a work of nonfiction. All people, locations, events, and situations are portrayed to the best of the author's memory.

Regalo Press
New York • Nashville
regalopress.com

Published in the United States of America
1 2 3 4 5 6 7 8 9 10

To my family

Table of Contents

Introduction

I still worry.

I wake up in the middle of the night and stare at the ceiling. Hot tears soak my pillow.

I don't cry over dying. I cry over missing: Violet's first ballet recital, Astrid's first basketball game or speech contest or science fair or tattoo, the rugged contours of John's hands as he holds mine. I cry over missing my pets' lives and their inability to understand why I'm gone.

It might not happen, of course. I might live to a happy old age, or I might get hit by a bus later today. The unknown doesn't bother me as much as the million realities of things I might miss.

That's life, though I suspect most people—at least people who haven't been forced to face mortality—don't spend much time thinking about it.

I measure the timeline of my life by individual animal lives. How many animal lives can I squeeze into my one small life?

Some have been long lives I've held in my hands, while others have been fleeting, in my care for weeks or months. When Emmett entered my world all those years ago, he tilted my axis.

It's an odd thing we humans do: We fall head over heels for an animal who becomes our sidekick, our companion, our friend. All the while, we know our lifeline extends further than theirs.

Maybe we love dogs so thoroughly because we know our time together is brief.

Loving a dog makes you a little more dog-like and a lot more human. You head out for hikes, you walk around the block, you snuggle under the covers, you spend quality time together while ignoring the loss that looms around the corner.

Yet, the day comes. It always does, and it's always too soon. Always.

You find yourself crying from a seemingly bottomless well. You see all the empty spaces: the place by the kitchen table where your dog sat each night hoping for little bites sneaked under the table, the corner of the sofa where he napped every afternoon because the sun hit it just right, the blanket at the foot of the bed that you can't bear to move or look at.

Those spaces echo with the emptiness.

You say goodbye to the dog who's been by your side—for maybe as long as two decades—and the habits and routines you've performed without thinking for those years suddenly appear in stark contrast to your dog-less life.

The cache of balls you discover when you rearrange your living room furniture guts you. Your pants remain fur-free and you find yourself missing the mess.

Somehow, for most of us, the time comes when those spaces are ready to be filled by the love of another animal. Another dog bounds in and brings that spirit that exists in no other animal on earth. The time comes to wash those balls and pick out a new bed and a new collar and a new companion.

A pet expands your world and your heart. Each time you say goodbye, they take a piece with them, yet somehow the empty space helps you love deeper and understand more.

As I think about my life, and its story arc, I wonder how many more I will welcome and love and understand and mourn. Ideally, I'm at about the halfway point in my own life—squarely middle aged. How many more dogs' lives might grace what time I have left?

I strive to be as dog-like as possible, living in and enjoying the moments I'm given. That fuels me and my writing. It is both the arc of my life and the arc of my work.

Dogs live in the moment; I live in my head. Writing gives me a way out. As Joan Didion said, "I write entirely to find out what I'm thinking, what I'm looking at, what I see and what it means. What I want and what I fear."

I write about dogs because I've found a subject that's endlessly fascinating, funny, and emotional.

The excitement of writing about dogs lies in the constantly evolving understanding of our best friends. The science astounds me. The discoveries rivet me. I love reading new research about the latest in dog behavior research or how functional magnetic resonance imaging (fMRI) demonstrates how a dog's brain reacts differently to the smell of his owner versus the smell of a hot dog. That stuff inspires me and lets me look at animals in a new light every day.

For those of us who live in our imaginations, who internalize the world, dogs serve as a grounding force. Dogs live for the moment. If they're tired, they sleep. If they're playful, they play. If they're hungry, they turn those sad puppy-dog eyes your way. If they're mad, they growl. Dogs demonstrate the power of simply being. They're never dishonest. They never overthink.

We're nearly to the point of welcoming another dog into our home. We are, for the moment, full up on cats, but there's a spot on the couch for another dog—an empty space in the bedroom for a pile of fur and paws. When that time arrives, when the dog appears, we'll throw ourselves into him or her fully, knowing that someday we'll say goodbye.

I don't want to arrive at the end of my life thinking, "But I have more left in me! I have more to give, more to write, more animals to help." I want to arrive at the end totally used up, with all my energy and all my ideas expended over my lifetime.

Thank goodness, then, that my love for dogs has helped fulfill my goal to live a full and vibrant life. After all, dogs are the best thing to happen to people.

Their bottomless capacity for forgiveness leaves me dumbfounded. From the lady walking down the road who yanks her dog forward instead of letting him smell something awesome to the outright physical abuse dogs suffer at the hands of men—they forgive.

Their enduring and endearing ability to find joy in the little things inspires me to look for more happiness each day. Their ability to improve any person's mood, and any situation, just by being present, is unparalleled.

We don't deserve dogs. Or, at least, dogs deserve for us to do better.

When I first started this book, I wanted to say how grateful I am that dogs can change the world, that I had dogs that changed my world. I wanted this to be the lasting testament to the boys that altered the tapestry of my life.

I wanted to tell my dogs' stories so they last forever, so I never have to say goodbye, so their memory doesn't disappear when I eventually do.

This is their story. Not mine.

It's only fair to put this right up front: Yes, the dog dies in this book. I wish it wasn't true, but it is. I don't like being blindsided by dogs dying in books, so there you go.

Every animal teaches us something—sometimes about ourselves, sometimes about the larger world in which we live. Or, I should say, each animal has the capacity to teach us, if only we have the capacity and willingness to listen. A dog can change the way you see the world. A dog can change the way you see yourself. If you're open to the possibilities, a dog will change your life.

We humans, we're capable of greatness. But somewhere along the line, we lose a bit of our spark. We make things difficult.

Humans overcomplicate things. Actually, we overcomplicate *everything*. Dogs keep things simple.

Dogs enjoy life. They don't need a trip that costs thousands of dollars to a theme park or a beach vacation. They don't need the latest brand-name collar or fancy spa treatments. They don't need a big house or a fancy car.

They need a puddle of sunshine for naps. They need a bowl full of food and another with fresh water. They need a toy and a person or two to play with them. They need a walk—not for torching calories, but for the sake of the walk itself. The sights. The feels. The smells. Especially the smells.

They need safety, security, a warm place to sleep, and a full tummy. Simple stuff.

People can treat each other terribly. Our lives have become so complicated that most of us go through it anxious or scared, to some degree, at all times. That doesn't bring out our best. It brings out our worst, "...the cruelty of frightened humans," as Richard Powers wrote in *The Overstory*.

Dogs bring us back down to earth. Back into ourselves.

We leash up our dog and lace up our sneakers. We head out on the sidewalk and travel the familiar roads around our home. We wave to our neighbors, to other dog walkers. We maybe even stoop down to pick up a piece of trash as we're picking up our dog's poop. We notice things that walkers without dogs don't. We see the houses that go up for sale and note that the new family must have little kids based on the bikes unloaded from the van—*let's be sure to bring them cookies*—and we see the elderly man down the road struggling to shovel his snow. But before we can help, another neighbor with a dog beats us to it and clears the driveway and sidewalks of not just his house, but ours, too.

Dogs get us outside our homes and inside our bodies.

When I run trails with Coop, my feet are firmly grounded with each step. I hear the birds chirping and the occasional hoot of an owl. I hear the *tap-tap-tap* of woodpeckers and the crunch of gravel under our feet. I hear all of it, accompanied by the jingle of Cooper's tags.

I see the leaves change, the subtle shift of the seasons. Everything is vibrant and green one day. The water gurgles in the creek, and I hear the ebb and flow of the cicadas calling from the trees. Then, moments later, we head out and I see tips of yellow and orange sprinkled throughout the tall branches, and I know on the next walk, everything will be a fiery red. Best of all, though, for me and Cooper anyway, is when all the leaves blanket the earth. The ground beneath our feet solidifies with the descending cold. Our breath clouds as we run.

I see winter arrive. We run through clear air under a slate-gray sky. Icy wisps of wind find their way into my coat, and patches of frozen leaves threaten to trip us up. Snow muffles our footfalls. It feels like there's no one else in the world but me and my dog.

I see Cooper slowing down, too. We spend all our time together, so sometimes the changes are too gradual for me to notice. Other times, though, I can see his stiff joints work against him as he jumps into bed at night. Or I see him snooze through fireworks or choose not to attack the vacuum (good boy!) or take an extra day to recover from a big run.

Those moments remind me: Our time is short. Far too short.

I love to picture the gnarly, spreading root systems that fan out beneath trees. I particularly love to imagine them underneath a perfectly manicured lawn. It's funny that people try to tame and trim and direct nature. Nature will always find its own way, and it will rarely be neat and orderly. It will rarely be manicured into perfectly groomed rows or spring up weed-free and ornamental. After all, as A.A. Milne wrote, "Weeds are flowers too, once you get to know them."

I think of myself as a weed. I'll find a way. It'll usually be messy. Gnarly. Under the surface. But I'll find it. My guides are not experts. My guides are my dogs, seeing me through it all. Sometimes I lead, sometimes I follow. No matter what, though, I find a way, led by my dogs.

I wrote this book to honor those of us who have all come to an agreement: The pain of loss is worth the price of love.

CHAPTER 1

What Makes a Dog, Anyway?

Hot puffs of air hit my face. I pulled the covers above my chin and nestled under the old, holey quilt. "Go lie down," I whispered. "It's too early."

A gentle *thud, thud, thud* answered me. I opened my eyes and peeked out of my blankets. We made eye contact. The thud sped up.

Lucas stood next to my side of the bed, his chin resting on my pillow. I rolled over and tried to drop back to sleep, but Lucas persisted.

I swung my legs out from under the covers, stretched, and stood. "Let's go, bud."

His hot breath on my face and his tail thumping my nightstand woke me every morning. And, every morning, I gave in to him.

Lucas raced downstairs to start his day at breakneck speed. His nails clattered across the hardwood floor as he shot down the steps. Even on three legs, he flew across the house faster than the other two dogs clambered out of bed.

Emmett, curled up in the middle of the chaise in the corner of my bedroom, yawned, stretched, scratched his ear, and peeled himself off his cozy spot. He ambled downstairs and waited by the back door.

Cooper, glued to his spot at the foot of the bed, watched and waited. When I came out of the bathroom and started down the steps, he finally jumped off the bed. Cooper would never do anything—even as simple as walking downstairs for breakfast—without waiting for me.

I opened the door to let the dogs out into the fenced-in backyard while I scooped coffee grounds and measured water into the coffee maker. By the time the pot finished brewing, the dogs were ready to come inside and gobble down their kibble, then commute with me back upstairs to the spare room converted into an office. The tiny space was stuffed with my desk, my desk chair, my books and notebooks, two dog beds, and a worn-through armchair. The boys tucked into their spots—Coop on the chair, Emmett and Lucas on each bed—and drifted back to sleep while I opened my laptop and started my workday.

Nearly 40,000 years of evolution had led to this—my three dogs and our sleepy morning routine.

That one evolutionary timeline had also led to three mismatched outcomes in my dogs. Emmett filled his thick, stout, muscular frame. Sized and shaped like a stereotypical pit bull, he oscillated between strong and chunky. Emmett's brindle fur wove together patches of dark brown with blond, caramel, and black everywhere except his all-white chest. Small, triangular ears poked out of his blocky head. Incongruous to the rest of his body, Emmett's feet and toes were small—almost dainty.

My husband, John, and I adopted Emmett less than a year after we married. A good Samaritan had picked Emmett up as an emaciated stray in the Virginia woods and took him to the county shelter. One night, a staff member forgot to lock his cage door, but Emmett waited in his crate all night and was discovered snoozing with the door open the next morning. Probably waiting for breakfast.

The staff at the shelter loved him so much they let him overstay his stray hold. Thankfully, a volunteer sprung him from the county shelter before his borrowed time ran out. He lived at Friends of Homeless Animals (FOHA) in Northern Virginia until we found him.

It was love at first sight. He barreled straight toward us, launched himself into my lap, and with a lick across my cheek, he made it clear: He was our dog.

Lucas arrived a year later. We had decided to adopt a friend for Emmett and found Lucas tucked into a kennel at an animal shelter in Washington, DC.

Shaped like a small German Shepherd, Lucas clocked in at about fifty pounds when we adopted him. His shelter card stated he was fully grown at about one to two years old, but needed to fill out due to starvation. Ultimately, he'd wind up many inches taller and a solid eighty pounds. Thick yellow fur covered his whole body except for his tail, which was wiry with black and brown hairs woven in with the yellow. Enormous ears shaped like handlebars stuck out from his soft face. He came to us skinny, limping, and terrified, especially of other dogs. His fear caused him to behave wildly half the time—lunging, snarling, snapping, biting—and the other half crouched behind an armchair, curled into himself, shut off from us.

Cooper came much later, the only one of the boys not adopted from a DC-area shelter. After we relocated from DC to Bloomington, Indiana, I volunteered for a pit bull advocacy organization based in Indianapolis and signed up to be a foster parent to dogs who needed a temporary home. I wanted to use my time to help dogs like Emmett, and I needed to find ways to make friends in our new home. So, I immersed myself in volunteer activities.

The first puppy we ever fostered started out as a fuzzy, squeaky, eight-week-old runt. He had an enormous puppy belly, bunny rabbit–soft red fur, and too-big ears that perched atop his head. He looked like a cartoon of a puppy instead of a real one. His tiny toenails clicked across the wood floors, and he made peeping sounds at John, begging to be picked up. John would tuck him into his sweater while he worked at his computer.

The moment that puppy curled up to sleep on top of Lucas, he became ours. We changed his name from Scooter to Cooper and removed our names from the foster list. The risk of adopting more puppies was too great.

Once Cooper joined the herd, we settled into a routine in our new home. I worked remotely doing the same job I held in DC—all while building a side business as a freelance writer. John worked long hours as a grad student at a lab on campus. For the vast majority of our time in Bloomington, I spent long days with just me and my boys.

Throughout my workday, Emmett slept soundly in his bed. Cooper padded around the house at my ankle. When I worked, he curled up in the armchair. When I went downstairs, he went downstairs. When I went to the bathroom, he waited for me at the sink.

Lucas, though, watched through upstairs and downstairs windows to ensure we weren't under attack. If he thought we were, he'd bark ferociously until the UPS guy left or the wind stopped blowing in a weird way. Then he'd pluck a toy from the wicker box in the living room and toss it in the air for himself while the other two slept the day away. Sometimes I wandered downstairs for a cup of coffee or a snack, and I found Lucas chewing an antler on the living room couch—the one place dogs weren't allowed—and he'd wag his tail while he slid off the cushions. "Always so naughty," I said, and kissed his enormous head.

The three dogs acted nothing alike: Lucas, always searching for fun or trouble; Emmett, stalwart and steady, unflappable and gentle; and Cooper, high-strung, anxious, and clingy.

How did their wild wolf ancestors' DNA turn and spin and change them into the couch-surfing, yogurt-loving mutts snoring around my desk?

I watched my boys and wondered: What made dogs *dogs*?

Despite their differences, all three were clearly *dogs*. Where did they come from, and how did they change from being wild and free to sharing our duvet and slurping puppy lattes from the drive-through?

Since I was building a freelance writing business, I decided to start researching those questions in detail. I launched a blog to chronicle the dogs' lives in our family and to discover more about how they think, feel, learn, and play—along with how they evolved to be our best friends. Most of us don't have pigs or pigeons or chinchillas curled up under the covers with us at night. So, why dogs?

As I tugged the thread to unravel the connection between dogs and humans, I sank deeper into the research and started to look at Emmett, Lucas, and Cooper in a whole new light.

Experts pretty much agree that dogs became dogs between 20,000 and 40,000 years ago. What isn't agreed on, though, is *how* they went from wolves to dogs. The prevailing theory suggests some brave wolves started hanging out on the outskirts of human camps because they could easily scavenge our leftovers. These wolves benefited from sticking close to us because hunting is dangerous and people are messy, so they could eat our garbage without putting their lives on the line. Meanwhile, our human ancestors benefited from the wolves' presence because, most likely, the wolves alerted them to predators approaching. Right off the bat, people and would-be dogs teamed up for their mutual benefit—kicking off the tens of thousands of years of evolution that eventually led to Lucas licking organic peanut butter out of a plastic puzzle toy.

After wolves started to brave the edges of human settlements, the next part of the story is debated among scientists. However, the general idea is that people, understanding the usefulness of partnering with wolves, selected the bravest and the friendliest to hang around inside their camps instead of keeping them on the outskirts. Those friendlier wolves then mated with each other and began to diverge from their wolf family tree.

This is where the research gets murky. Some scholars believe wolf evolution continued until we ended up with the Puggles and Doodles of today. Others believe an interim species emerged—not quite a wolf anymore, but not yet a dog—and our pet dogs descended from that transitional canine instead of directly from wolves. Regardless, we've loved dogs for a long time. The oldest discovered fossil of a dog—a true dog, a species separate from a wolf—dates back 14,000 years.

Around 7,000 years ago, dogs were pretty much everywhere, but they didn't live among humans like dogs today, who snooze in sunspots and chew squeaky toys on orthopedic bolster beds. They were more free-ranging but still provided a service—safety—to the humans nearby. Even then, our ancient ancestors valued their relationships with their dogs enough to be buried with them.

Dogs' evolution veered off this linear path when we modern humans started breeding them purposefully for skills that came more naturally to some dogs—like hunting or herding or guarding, or for specific appearances. Dog breeds only emerged within the last few centuries. In fact, researcher Brian Hare wrote in *Survival of the Friendliest*, "European dog breeds have a surprisingly recent origin. People cultivated them during the Victorian age, when the physical appearance of a dog became more important than the job the dog was supposed to perform." Dog shows began in the late nineteenth century so fanciers could choose dogs to breed with their own to create these breeds and their "pure" bloodlines.

Before there were specific breeds, there were dogs. When you unravel their evolutionary story, it's remarkable and humbling to realize dogs evolved specifically as our partners. They came into being because some traits made them better allies and friends to early humans. Our histories and our ancestries are intertwined so inextricably that we can't separate our lifelines from theirs over the past 20,000 years.

We are buddies on an evolutionary scale.

Depending on which organization you ask, there are as many as 400 different dog breeds around now, and still more extinct. Most dogs aren't even a specific breed. *Smithsonian* magazine described dogs as "close genetic relatives with an incredibly diverse range of appearances and behaviors." Yet, anyone can look at each of those 400 dogs and identify it as a dog, regardless of appearance or behavior. Despite their disparities in features like size, coat, temperament, and bark, a Dachshund, a Saint Bernard, a Dalmatian, and a Sheepdog all share most of their DNA. Everyone, even a tiny child, can look at any breed and identify it as a dog.

DNA tests for dogs are commercially available for any pet owner who wants to dig into their pup's ancestry. Through the contact form on my dog blog, two of the test manufacturers reached out about their at-home DNA test kits, so I decided to swab Lucas with one and Cooper with the other. Lucas's breed seemed to be German Shepherd mixed with who-knows-what, while I figured Cooper's was straightforward since his mother's lineage was already known to us.

I swabbed Lucas's cheeks and mailed everything to the company. Shortly after, we received the results—and were shocked.

Lucas's DNA, we discovered, was predominantly German Shepherd Dog (GSD), which was no surprise. One half of his DNA, contributed by one of his two parents, showed only GSD, going all the way back to his grandparents. He strongly resembled a GSD, and this was what I guessed would show up on his test.

Where the shock came in: His other half was provided by a parent who was a Saint Bernard-Boxer mix. I looked at him and couldn't see either of those breeds clearly, but the geneticist could. When I spoke with her about his test, she told me his ears have the "airplane effect" because he has a base of cartilage contributed from his boxer ancestor, but that his size comes from the other two breeds.

I also asked her about Lucas's yellow coat. It struck me that neither German Shepherds nor Saint Bernards are known to be yellow. Yellow, she told me, is a recessive gene in dog coats. It takes two copies of the gene, instead of a single copy of a dominant gene, to create a yellow dog. As it turns out, all three breeds that made up Lucas's DNA have a yellow gene. Black is a dominant trait, and in Lucas it showed up in his "mask," or the black on his face, something common in all three of his ancestors' breeds.

But what did the German Shepherd/Saint Bernard/boxer combo mean for his periodic aggression and fear? Did those breed-specific pieces of his DNA impact how he responded and recovered from his triggers?

Purposeful breeding focused on tweaking aspects of the prey drive to create dogs who worked how we needed them to: hunting, retrieving, herding, guarding, and so on. Humans have been incredibly specific in our breeding process. We've bred dogs to increase the frequency or intensity of a specific behavior for each individual breed. Think of a Terrier chasing rats, a Collie herding sheep, or a Spaniel retrieving birds. When you shake up those traits in a single dog, the result is a mix and match of behaviors potentially much closer to the "natural" state of a dog.

In other words, as the geneticist told me, mixed-breed dogs become a jack of all trades, master of none. Lucas boasted a good combo of his ancestors' traits without excelling at any, but nothing about Lucas—his appearance or his behavior—was a fluke. It was all predestined by this unique set of chromosomes.

Cooper's DNA test was far simpler and less surprising. His lineage included a mother whose line was entirely American Staffordshire Bull Terrier, which we were already aware of since we knew who his mama dog was. In fact, his maternal side remained consistent through his great grandparents. The father? Well, Cooper's father's DNA was already so blurred, the test stated "mixed breed" without any single breed's DNA emerging.

Like Lucas and Cooper, most dogs are mixes of many breeds swirled together to create another unique set of traits that are still completely identifiable as "dog."

The outside characteristics, like fur and tails, gives us a clue. But even dogs' external traits range from fur like Lucas's, so thick I could paste together all the hair I brushed out of him each week into a second Lucas, or thin and wiry like Cooper's. Tails can curl like a Pug or hang long and fluffy like a Pyrenees.

Same goes for ears. From the droopy Basset Hound to the perky Bull Terrier, anyone who loves dogs can see an ear and want to give it a rub.

Body types can vary dramatically, too. Some dogs evolved into bodies built for difficult work: livestock-guarding dogs use their hulking forms to safeguard vulnerable herds of livestock. Others, like the Border Collie, come in smaller, faster bodies designed through human intervention to zip around huge flocks of sheep or geese and keep them all together. Other dogs, like my mom's little fluff ball, a Shih Tzu mix named Otto, were built for resting on laps and snoring in the shade.

Even though Emmett's strong, thick body radiated strength, his disposition meant he never actually wanted to use any of his strength…unless he was scaling countertops for a pan of biscuits. Like us humans, the way a dog looks is such a small percentage of the dog's genes. Even though I can see a Great Dane and a Chinese Crested and know both are dogs, what makes them a dog has little to do with their appearance—disparate as they are.

Physical traits—the fur, the ears, the muscle and sinew or fat, the build, the scale, the shape of the head and the thickness of the neck, the length of the tail—take up half a dozen spots on a dog's genome. In people, hundreds of variants create our physical differences.

There's a chemical composition, too, contributing to the makeup of a dog. For instance, oxytocin—a hormone in humans and dogs—is responsible for creating a sense of trust and empathy, for helping us understand each other when communicating, and for establishing a connection between mother and infant. Oxytocin creates bonds not just between humans, but between humans and dogs. Our brains and our dogs' brains do something amazing together: We create an oxytocin loop. No other cross-species partnership does this. Researchers at Azabu University in Sagamihara, Japan, discovered that as we gaze into the eyes of our dogs and they gaze into ours, we both experience an increase in oxytocin—as much as a 130 percent increase in dogs and a 300 percent increase in their owners. As a result, we often love each other even more. As simplistic as it sounds, this biological response to looking into each other's eyes may have been a major factor in our coevolution. Studies show the near relatives of dogs and humans—wolves and chimps, respectively—don't experience the same oxytocin increase; in fact, they may avoid eye gaze entirely. Like human moms and their infants, our eye contact with our dogs makes us both feel safe, secure, connected, and loved.

What makes this especially amazing is that the same doesn't hold true for species-species eye gaze, at least not for dogs. If Lucas locked eyes with an unfamiliar dog, we knew we needed to break his focus, or a fight was likely. If Lucas locked eyes with Emmett or Cooper, we knew a playfight—one that knocked lamps off of side tables and sent chairs flying—was imminent. If I caught them fast enough and sent them outside, they'd wrestle around our backyard, hunks of grass and mud flying while our poor plants were trampled. While they enjoyed the romp, the eye gaze that sparked the playfight was certainly not the same as the joy-flooded, calming oxytocin loop they created with us.

Then there are other characteristics, the hard-to-quantify traits that make a dog a dog. Some of these traits emerge from a chromosome, others from conditioning, and the rest from the unique brew of DNA and environment. When we think of dogs, what traits make them who they are?

Loyalty, of course, makes a dog a dog. Dogs seem to be wired for partnership with us, making us the luckiest species on earth in my opinion. Our dogs deserve to have their tens of thousands of years of genetically programmed loyalty honored and respected. They cast their lots with people, and people are imperfect—even cruel sometimes.

Protectiveness makes a dog a dog, though with enormous degrees of variation. Think of the stereotypical junkyard dog left outside to bark and scare—and even attack—people who want to steal the junk they guard with their lives. Some dog breeds emerged to fill the role of family or flock protector. Anatolian Shepherds protect livestock and guard their animals against predators in Turkey. Rottweilers, ancient dogs descended from those of the Roman legions, drive cattle and serve in police and military forces. They're often recommended as family protectors. But almost all dogs protect in some capacity; they bark and growl at threats, both imagined and real. Lucas flung himself at windows and doors, barking and lunging to keep us safe from Girl Scouts selling cookies, leaves blowing across the sidewalk, and all manner of door-to-door salespeople. Had a real threat ever emerged, he was ready.

Affection, too, makes a dog a dog. But just like people, the amount of affection each dog wants to give and receive varies enormously. Some dogs don't love to be petted. Others want a full-body massage every night. We once fostered a high-energy puppy named Molly who spent every waking minute running, jumping, playing, skittering, and wrestling with Cooper. But as soon as night fell, she wanted a soft lap to curl up in—she was the size of a cat—and gentle rubs until bedtime. Emmett, on the far end of the attention-seeking spectrum, needed constant affection, and if no one was touching him at a given moment, he walked over and pushed his face underneath someone's hand to solicit attention. Cooper fell somewhere in the middle, needing lots of love and affection from people he trusted, but avoiding the touch of everyone else.

Love makes a dog a dog, though not the unconditional kind we attribute to our furballs. Science shows it's much more nuanced than a bottomless pit of starry-eyed devotion. It's a mistake to believe dogs love unconditionally. Dogs are unconditionally loyal, sacrificing their own joy to follow the instructions of the person who holds the other end of their leash. But love? Love comes when an owner doesn't ask their dog to sacrifice their joy for obedience. Love comes from trust, and it comes from security. When they have those foundations, dogs feel pretty darn happy with us. Their brains prove it.

Scientists at Emory University trained dogs—future assistance dogs, all under a year old—to withstand the stress of an MRI machine. They used functional magnetic resonance imaging (fMRI) to map dogs' brain activities when exposed to dog and human smells. The study found that when the dogs smelled their owners' unique scents, it sparked the "reward center" of their brains. They preferred the whiff of their people over anything or anyone else. Even hot dogs.

In Budapest, other scientists conducted a similar study. They trained dogs to withstand ten minutes in an MRI machine while listening to 200 different human and dog sounds. In this study, researchers isolated the part of the dogs' brains that registered sounds and found it works exactly like our "voice area" does. This part of our brain was only discovered in humans in the 1990s and it serves to not only help us regulate the pitch and tone of our voice, but to recognize the patterns and rhythms of the sounds other people make—an essential element of effective social interactions. Turns out, dogs have a similar area—and the study showed dogs like the sound of their people's voice.

Our smells and our voices make our dogs happy. We make our dogs happy. It doesn't take a huge leap to think our dogs love us as we love them.

Additional studies from Yale, MIT, and Duke indicate the emotional centers of dogs' brains work like those in human toddlers. Anyone who's ever cared for a toddler knows how complex their emotions are, how deeply they think and feel.

Many dog lovers know this already. None of this research is likely to surprise lifelong dog lovers or small children with a canine best friend. We intuit the depths of our dogs' thoughts and feelings, and we know how individual and unique each dog is. Why spend a tremendous amount of time, money, and manpower to test something we already know?

In part, it's human nature to attempt to unravel every secret, to understand everything hidden to us. It's also part animal welfare. When we know how an animal thinks and feels, we should be inspired to treat that animal more humanely.

Even in some places around the United States, many believe an "outside dog" isn't a huge deal, but no one would ever have an "outside toddler." Their brains process loneliness and loss and love the same way, so what's the difference?

Or imagine your three-year-old has a potty accident. Do you push her face into it? Of course not. The thought is horrifying. Yet, traditional dog trainers suggest you do that while house-training your puppy.

If you've ever loved a dog, or even if you've only ever met a dog, you've seen how full their personalities are. Part of my responsibility to my dogs is to allow them to be themselves, to enjoy what makes them happy.

I've met owners and trainers who trained the uniqueness right out of their dogs. During the years Emmett worked as a therapy dog, we often found ourselves with another handler and her pair of dogs who sat by her ankles, waiting to be cued. Even when the dogs had the chance to get some wiggles out, to run around and sniff, they sat and awaited instruction.

Those dogs never seemed happy. While the other dogs around them wiggled their loose bodies and wagged their tails, those two sat unmoving, watching and waiting to be told what to do. My dogs, while wildly imperfect, have always been happy. They're trained, yes, but they have agency. They're free to make choices. My goal in training is to teach them to make more good choices—like waiting on their bed as I open the front door—than bad choices, like eating stray sandwiches discovered under park benches.

None of these individual elements, the internal or the external, really make a dog a dog, however. Instead, it's the magical combination of it all: their adorable appearance, genetically crafted to make us swoon; their loyal, protective nature, combined with the right degree of gentleness and affection; the partnership that emerges between us; and the reliability of a friend at home who's always happy to see you, who loves you no matter how you look or feel, who stands by your side in the sun or the rain, who doesn't care what you're wearing or how far you've climbed the corporate ladder or how well you speak in public.

To your dog, you're perfect.

The elements that make a dog a dog become sharp and pronounced on the individual level. My childhood dog, a poorly bred Bichon named Sparky who we purchased from a Baltimore-area mall in the mid-1980s, chased airplanes and his tail. He preferred kibble to people food, and even then it had to be kibble in a specific size, shape, and color—otherwise he left it in his bowl. I remember my mom calling the Purina customer service line to complain on his behalf. Despite his quirks, he let me lay my head on his back and nestle into his fluffy white fur after a hard day at school. I told him my secrets, and he snuggled me in return.

Emmett's elements made him the perfect therapy dog. His combination of steadiness, gentleness, and a dash of playfulness enabled him to work with the adolescent residents of a mental health facility, all of whom had already suffered in their young lives. Until his retirement, he provided constant and stalwart attention, affection, and fun.

Cooper's elements—intensity, loyalty, intelligence, patience, and strength in a sinewy frame—turned him into the perfect companion and big brother to our two humans, Violet and Astrid. Cooper grew into the ideal running partner, following me down any path at any pace for any duration. Of course, those traits could've been his downfall in someone else's hands. Cooper would do what I asked of him, including running, until he dropped. He protected the girls as babies and guarded them into toddlerhood. His loyalty genes are strong, which contributed to his naturally high-strung anxious personality.

Lucas's formative experience altered his inborn elements. His early life wired his brain to fear people and avoid partnership. His nature was fun-loving, mischievous, gentle, and fierce, but it took us a while to see those traits. Once we did, we were able to coax out his true disposition and overcome—at least a little—the impact his environment had on his genetics.

We humans have a tremendous responsibility to our dogs. What makes a dog a dog is what makes them so easily exploited and abused. Not every dog lands in a home with a person who identifies and cares for their individual characteristics. It's on us animal lovers to honor dogs for who they are and to demand that they're treated humanely.

Training and working together for a task takes our evolutionary alliance and turns it into a friendship. For people all over the world, their partnership with their dog means their families eat or stay safe. The dogs work—not *for* their people, but *with* their people. They herd, hunt, retrieve, and guard.

These relationships keep food on the table. But these types of relationships, and that type of training, isn't what most of us do.

For most of us, we teach our pets how to stay safe in our human world. It's a big job because we live in a complicated, confusing world to dogs. To a dog, eating garbage makes sense: It smells good and tastes awesome. To a dog, barking at the wind as it blows leaves across the sidewalk makes sense: He's protecting his family from something he doesn't understand and, therefore, might be dangerous. To a dog, shoving his nose into your houseguest's crotch makes sense: It smells interesting and tells him everything he needs to know about your friend.

We teach our dogs not to eat garbage and to stop barking on cue. The crotch sniffing can be a tougher habit to break—I mean, to your dog, it's *right there* at nose level—but your dog can learn to resist the impulse. Ultimately, most of us are training our dogs to behave and to stay safe.

Some concepts couldn't possibly make sense to a dog, but they learn to operate within our constructs. For instance, sidewalks. Sidewalks are a plain, boring strip of poured concrete cutting through patches of fragrant grass. Why walk in a straight line along this unwavering thread when you can dash and dart and sniff and twirl and backtrack and pee on all the stuff *around* the scratchy, hard path?

But dogs can't understand our line of thinking. Dart too far one way and you might end up in traffic. Too far the other way and the mean lady down the road who doesn't want anyone stepping on her grass might come out and scream at you. Or a bike rider might smash into you. Or your leash might trip a runner.

Over time, our dogs do learn to walk nicely by our sides along these safe, boring sidewalks. We can train them to do that.

We can't train them to enjoy it as much as they enjoy meandering and sniffing. To honor our partnership, we can search for a balance of meeting their needs and our own.

Sometimes, finding a balance is easy: When Emmett first came home, we took him out a few times a day for what we called his constitutional. Emmett's constitutional was dedicated to getting him to poop. He would hold it and hold it and hold it because he realized as soon as he went, we walked home. So he faked the movements—as if he was getting ready to go in one spot, then he'd straighten up and prance to another spot, then he'd wander in a totally different direction. I felt frustrated with Em taking ages to poop. He seemed frustrated to be rushed along. For the sake of our relationship, we needed a solution. John and I lived in a condo, so there wasn't the option of a backyard. We decided to split his walks into "poop walks" and "sniff walks." Sniff walks entered the park and meandered in any direction he chose. He got two of those every day. Poop walks happened on the strip of scrub grass alongside our building and were short trips simply to empty him out. He caught on quickly, and balance was restored.

Sometimes, finding a balance is difficult. What do we do with all the dogs born to unwanted litters? What do we do with our overcrowded shelters crammed full of strays, of puppies and dogs waiting for a home?

Over tens of thousands of years, we turned wolves into dogs, and we bred and overbred them until they started to rely on us for survival instead of the other way around.

And that's where my story began.

Not with Lucas waking me up far too early every morning with his hot breath and his tail thumps—but with Emmett, locked in a kennel at an animal shelter. Waiting.

CHAPTER 2

Where Dogs Come From (and Why It Matters)

In the beginning there was Emmett.

Although we didn't know it yet.

John and I married in the fall, bought a condo in the spring, and set out to adopt a dog by the summer. We didn't yet own a kitchen table or chairs, but we knew: a dog was first.

We drove to Friends of Homeless Animals (FOHA) in Northern Virginia to meet the dogs we'd stalked on their website. We talked with the adoption coordinator about our lifestyle and what we were looking for: a dog who could go anywhere with us—from camping to a downtown festival—and who could be good with kids someday. We didn't want a dog we left at home to sleep on the couch all day; we wanted a dog to accompany us on our adventures.

"You need to meet Emmett," she said.

We walked him—or more accurately, he dragged us—around the facility to spend time getting to know one another, but it was hardly necessary. We knew he was our dog; he knew we were his family. We arrived back at the main office and filled in our application.

John and I lived in Columbia Heights, a bustling neighborhood in downtown Washington, DC, so we figured it would take Em a while to adjust. He was, by all accounts, a rural dog. But he hopped right into the back seat of our Saturn and rode for several minutes gazing out the window. Then, Emmett leaned forward, placed his head on the armrest between me and John, and fell asleep.

Emmett awoke at a red light at 14th and Connecticut Avenue, a crowded intersection filled with people during a busy Thursday lunch rush. He looked around. We thought he might panic at the dramatic change—falling asleep in the woods, waking up in the city—but he put his head back down. He sighed. He dozed off again. I reached over and scratched his ears.

We pulled into the parking garage of our building and led him to the elevator. Em took it all in stride, wagging his tail as his head swiveled and his nose twitched as he absorbed these new surroundings. He didn't even balk as the elevator doors swished shut and took us up to our floor.

Once inside our condo, we sat on the couch with Emmett on the floor between our legs. John and I looked at each other. We looked at Emmett. He tilted his head back and looked at us.

Emmett wagged.

"Now what?" I asked John.

As kids, both John and I lived with dogs. I grew up with Sparky—that loveable, lazy, picky eating Bichon. He passed away when I was in junior high and was followed by a pair of English Springer Spaniels, Lennon and Rutherford. John's mom took in a Shepherd mix named Smithers when John was a high schooler. Throughout our combined experiences, we were never the ones responsible for the care of the pups. Our parents were. Those dogs lived on the periphery of our lives. We were young, and they weren't our everything. They were part of our story, but not the narrative.

We both loved dogs, though. We knew we wanted a dog and had planned for this adoption immediately after our marriage. Now we had a dog at our feet and no clue what to do with him. So, we laced up our sneakers, clipped his brand-new nylon leash to his collar, and set off for the first of thousands of walks around Meridian Hill Park and our Columbia Heights neighborhood.

Two days later, Emmett yanked me across the slippery PetSmart linoleum. We entered the training ring.

"This is Emmett," Je'ree said. "He's new. Let's all give him a little space while we get to know him." Our human classmates eyed him and shifted themselves and their dogs to the plastic chairs across the ring.

We started a basic obedience class—taught by my best friend and professional dog trainer, Je'ree Hamlet-Nelson. She and I worked together for years at The National Geographic Society, and we bonded over our shared love of our dogs. Her dog, an enormous German Shepherd named Wookie, helped "teach" the class and became a mentor to Emmett, who we quickly realized knew nothing. What he lacked in knowledge, he made up for in gusto. He threw his sixty-five-pound muscular frame into each task with such force that he regularly knocked me down.

"We need to teach him to walk," Je'ree said.

Emmett flung himself across the ring while John tried to lure him to "heel."

"We need to teach him to sit," she said as Emmett jumped into my stomach, knocking the wind out of me for the fifth time that session.

We needed to teach him everything. He embodied the bull-in-a-china-shop cliché. He barreled through our first class so forcefully that our classmates inched further and further away over the course of the hour. Eventually we were on one side of the ring with Em and they were on the other side with their dogs.

Later in the summer, Emmett's beginner's certificate eked out, we languished in the DC humidity with long, slow walks around Meridian Hill Park and leisurely dinners with our neighbors.

Each week, we gathered in someone's condo, on a rooftop patio or a grassy courtyard. Everyone brought a dish or drinks, and we shared a meal together. If we ate on the roof or in the courtyard, we brought Emmett. If not, we stuffed a food toy for him and practiced working on his separation anxiety.

Because Emmett did not want to be away from us. Ever. Thankfully, John worked from home, though we did occasionally have to both leave at the same time. And when that happened—at least before we had training and management in place—Emmett destroyed our condo. So, each time we left home, even to take the elevator down to the lobby to collect a package or food delivery, we asked Em to go to his bed. We gave him the food-stuffed toy. We said, "Be good, Emmett. I love you. I'll be right back." As we closed the front door, we could see him on his bed, puzzling over his toy.

Our neighbors told us—kindly at first, then with increasing frustration—he cried for an hour or two at the door every time we left. After his crying bouts ended, he found ways to keep himself busy and express his anxiety: chewing the frame around the door, devouring his dog bed, digging into the drywall, and pulling everything off the kitchen counters.

One night, we dashed over to a friend's apartment to drop off some mail and didn't go through the whole routine of stashing everything in sight, putting him on his bed, and making a food toy. We were only going to be gone a minute, we reasoned, and were just a few doors down. The quick visit turned into an impromptu long conversation, but we didn't hear any crying or suspicious sounds from under our door.

When we returned home, we discovered my purse, which I kept on a high ledge in our kitchen, chewed open on the floor. *How on earth did he jump so high?* we asked ourselves as we cleaned up the mess.

"Oh, my God." I lifted the chewed-up side of a plastic Advil bottle in my hand. We scoured the room. No other plastic pieces. No pills.

I called the emergency vet. They asked how many pills the container held and how many were left. "I have no clue," I said. "It's a travel-sized bottle, but I don't know if it was even opened. They're all gone."

Advil is incredibly toxic to dogs. Even a single dose of Advil can cause a dog to go into renal failure.

"Bring him in right away," they said, so we sped to the twenty-four-hour veterinary hospital. We rushed him in, and they took him straight back.

A sleepy-looking vet came into the exam room and explained what was happening: They had induced vomiting, and we would give him activated charcoal at home until it was all out of him. Book a follow-up exam in a couple days, the vet said. "And, Emmett, no more self-medicating!"

Poor Emmett stumbled into the room. He saw us and wagged. He flopped down, exhausted from his bouts of vomiting. We drove him home in silence. John and I both felt the crash as adrenaline left our bodies and relief washed over us. Emmett was going to be okay. He snored the entire way back, already having forgotten the ordeal. He trotted from the car to the elevator and from the elevator to our front door, wagging his tail and sniffing the hallway for our friends.

While that was our first trip to the emergency vet, it certainly wasn't our last. In fact, it was merely a blip on the radar of things Emmett would go on to ingest. But it was the first panic, the first time we thought something terrible could happen to our boy, the first time his mortality and our responsibility to him sunk in.

Emmett's separation anxiety continued, and despite ongoing training and management plans, he still tried to dig out of our condo through the wall. So, when another trainer suggested we get Emmett a dog—a friend to keep him company—we jumped in the car and drove to the Washington Animal Rescue League (WARL), now known as the Humane Rescue Alliance. I had recently written an article on assignment about their extensive facility and the innovative ways they were trying to make life easier for shelter dogs. I knew we'd find the right dog for Emmett at WARL, though it didn't occur to me to look for the right dog for *us*.

John watched a pile of puppies while I wandered the rows of dogs. I paused at the door of the saddest looking dog in the shelter. Lucas, splayed on a cot, ignored the people passing his window. He wasn't asleep; he'd just turned his head to the side so as not to see the flow of people outside. The other dogs clamored at their doors, jumping up and wagging at the passersby. Lucas seemed oblivious.

I watched him for a few seconds. He lifted his head, locked eyes with me, heaved a sigh, and turned away. He looked so utterly sad the moment our eyes met, like he was almost ready to give up.

That was it for me. My heart ached for him. I called John over. "This dog," I said.

We spoke with a volunteer who told us they didn't think Lucas would fit in a home with an existing dog. "He's too selective about dogs," they said. "That's why he's housed alone."

We put in an application anyway.

Weeks passed. We heard nothing. We started to look for other dogs. We visited the FOHA website daily. We planned to visit the city shelter when, finally, a volunteer from WARL called us: Our application was approved for Lucas, pending a meet and greet with Emmett. They weren't sure Lucas could get along with another dog. "He can get along with Emmett," John told the volunteer because, we knew, Emmett got along with everyone.

We drove Em to the shelter, and if we had any sense whatsoever, we would've realized the depth of Lucas's issues by the number of shelter staff they sent with us to monitor their meeting. Instead, we focused on the boys—our boys—and their first interaction. They dashed around a little play yard, peed on everything, sniffed, and circumnavigated each other. At one point, Lucas put his head across the back of Emmett's neck. Emmett growled and gave him a push, something we'd never seen him do before.

"Don't worry. That was a totally appropriate interaction," the staff trainer said. "Lucas was rude. Emmett told him no, and Lucas listened." She paused. "I think they'll get along just fine."

Of course, for a long, long while, Emmett was the only dog Lucas got along with, though we wouldn't understand the full scope of Lucas's problems for some time. We had our hearts set on getting him to his new home.

Lucas, however, didn't want to get in the car.

He dug his paws into the pavement. He scrambled away from the open back seat door. He kicked and writhed and resisted every attempt to get him into the car. Meanwhile, Emmett sat in his seat, watching and waiting. Still, Lucas wouldn't budge. In the end, he flattened himself like a pancake and refused to move. His front and back legs splayed, and he pressed himself into the cement, averting his eyes.

We had no choice: We picked him up, John on the front and me on the rear, and we shoehorned him into the back seat. As soon as the door clicked shut, he opened his mouth and began to drool. We cracked the window so he could gulp fresh air, but by the time we arrived home, slobber caked the back window, the fabric of the back seat, and the entire back of my headrest. Even Emmett was drenched in Lucas's drool.

Like the first day we bought Emmett home, we started with a walk. We took them for individual walks, then combined walks. We kept them on leash in the condo at first, but by the time they ate dinner side by side later in the evening, the two were connected. A pair. As different from each other as apples and Volkswagens but somehow connected.

Lucas relied on Emmett for cues on how to behave. We watched him let Emmett go first in all things, and slowly, the two of them found equilibrium. Lucas demanded a lot, sometimes everything. Emmett demanded little, just some food and affection. The yin and yang of their relationship surprised me because I expected more primal responses and less nuance. But in the end, it came down to a give and take.

We joked that Emmett needed to teach Lucas "how to dog"—but it wasn't far from the truth.

After the first day home, Lucas shut down. While the shock of a new place and a new canine companion likely pushed him through that first day with us, we didn't yet know or understand the language of a highly sensitive, reactive dog. On the second day, he curled up behind the armchair in our living room, and there he stayed until mealtime or walks. He never wanted pets and never wagged his tail. He lunged at dogs. He shrank from people. Everything scared him: bikes and strollers, plastic bags, car horns and car doors, the television.

I started buying books about dogs, dog training, and dog behavior—anything I thought might help me unravel his fears. We enrolled in Je'ree's basic obedience class again. We re-enrolled Emmett, too, not only for the bonding, but because he needed the refresher.

One afternoon, on a bright, early summer Saturday, I walked Lucas and John walked Emmett. We walked the half block to Meridian Hill Park, to cover the route we knew inside and out. Anticipating foot traffic and knowing blind spots would become the key to survival with Lucas.

Before we hit the crosswalk, our next-door neighbor turned his car down the street.

"Hey, guys!" he yelled through the open window, his arm waving.

Lucas bolted.

He startled so quickly and so forcefully, I had no time to react. Somehow I held onto the leash, but in the process of him bolting and me holding on tight, he yanked me directly into the metal "No Parking" sign on the corner. I fell into the road, scraping the signpost the whole way down. John ran over and grabbed Lucas's leash while I pulled myself up. Tears streamed down my face. My injuries weren't significant—a scrape flared on my cheek and small cuts riddled my arms—but I barely noticed them at first. My chest ached and my stomach churned. I cried from the utter hopelessness I felt in that moment.

What is the matter with him? What can we do?

Over the next couple days, my arm puffed up and bruises bloomed. At the peak—my arm greeny-purple, scabbed, and swollen—I had my thirty-day review at my new job. "What happened to you?" my boss asked.

"My dog," I answered hopelessly.

Months passed. Lucas rarely wagged. He never wanted to snuggle.

What does he want?

I asked myself this question so many times, through so many tears.

Emmett sailed through life on charm. He never thought about much. Once he got over his separation anxiety, he barreled from one thing to the next and bounced back instantly after any setback. Lucas did nothing so easygoing as all that. He was hyperaware of and sensitive to *everything*, and he didn't bounce back. He reacted until he retreated.

We loved Lucas. We loved every perfect and every flawed part of him, and we committed to help him dismantle his fear. I just had no idea how. Not yet.

One night, a few months after he came home, Lucas and Emmett began to play together—and once they started, they never, ever stopped. The invitation to play pulled Lucas out from behind the armchair. Emmett would give a play bow or waggle a rope toy in his direction. Lucas would pop out from behind the chair. They'd both launch up on their hind legs and start WWE in our living room. They were both about seventy pounds—ultimately, Lucas would add another ten and Emmett would lose five to settle at their healthy adult weights—and our condo was tiny: 750 square feet. All John and I could do was tuck our legs up on the couch and wait for them to run out of steam.

At first, John and I worried it would turn into a fight. Dogs playing can certainly sound vicious. Flashes of teeth and growls accompany their games, and they alternate between pinning each other down and chasing each other around. With Emmett and Lucas—and most typical dogs—we could rely on them to regulate their own play. They excel at correcting one another and communicating when it's time to stop or to go. After our initial concern, we realized they policed their play better than we ever could, so we just let them go. Until our downstairs neighbor began coming up to ask us to please, please make them stop wrestling.

Then Lucas began his "midnight madness." Late each night, I'd settle in with a book or John and I would watch a show. Emmett tucked himself into his bed in the corner. Suddenly, seemingly out of nowhere, Lucas would spring up and run laps around our condo. He jumped on the couch and woofed, then bounced off, sprinted around the kitchen, dashed into the bedroom and onto the bed, where he twirled a couple times, then sprang off and into another round of living room laps and woofs. This continued nightly. We thought something was wrong. Emmett thought he was nuts. Lucas, though, was beginning to create his own fun.

Researchers call Lucas's behavior "frenetic random activity periods," or FRAPs. It means exactly that: a seemingly random burst of energy that drives the dog to zoom around. FRAPs are called "the zoomies," too, and they're incredibly common (and hilarious) in puppies. For Lucas, it almost seemed like after a day of walks, wrestling, and chewing, he still had a bit of energy, and he was committed to expending it before he got tucked into bed. So, he'd zoom. Or FRAP. The rest of us would tuck our legs up onto the couch or move to the kitchen table. Eventually, he'd tucker himself out and head to bed.

One night, the boys started to cuddle together on a great big dog bed. Every night thereafter, we tucked them into their own beds—one in each corner of the living room—but by morning they were snuggled together, sound asleep in the big bed by the door.

One day, almost three months after we adopted him, Lucas wagged at us when we came home. Soon after, he picked up toys and started to play tug and fetch with us. He asked for cuddles and rested his chin on our legs. If he wanted attention, he pawed me with his enormous feet.

There he is, I'd think as he wagged his tail while we tugged two ends of a rope. Then we'd open our front door, and he'd retreat back inside himself.

We met with several trainers who gave Lucas a label: aggressive. One trainer wanted us to wrap a pinching device around his neck made of plastic alligator teeth, and each time he acted out, we were to pop the collar to close the teeth around his throat.

Since when does hurting someone cure their fear?

We sought other answers and continued to work with the help of Je'ree and Wookie. We knew he was terrified, and no one wants to be terrified.

That was our foundation. We knew he was in there. We knew how fun-loving and playful he could be. We saw it in his daily interactions with Emmett. It was just hard for him to access that part of himself with anyone other than Em. The defenses he built were so thick and so high and so dense, it took monumental effort to dismantle them.

I was exhausted, but determined.

And I was finally starting to grasp the impact my dogs were having on my life and my worldview. To understand them exactly as they really were was beginning to help me understand myself.

And then there were three.

We picked up Scooter on Halloween morning, a year and a half after adopting Lucas. Scooter's pudgy puppy belly distended as he waddled around the crate trying to get comfortable. He whimpered, settled, then whimpered some more. A bunny-soft layer of fuzz covered his body, and tiny black toenails poked out of round paws. His ears, much too big for his body, drooped forward, the tips resting on the top of his head. "Do you think they'll stay like that?" my mom asked. I hoped so.

He arrived at our house as a foster dog. A few days before, the coordinator for a pit bull rescue called to ask if I could foster a puppy. A litter had been dumped at a low-cost clinic and needed temporary homes until they were ready for adoption. John and I knew people who fostered and admired their life-saving commitment. We wanted to try. We wanted to help little buddies get whole or well again while awaiting their forever family. So, Scooter came home with us, our first—and last—foster puppy.

On his first day, he tested out all the toys, rushed around the house, snuggled with John, and tried to get the big dogs to play with him as often as possible. Emmett and Lucas hesitated at first. I wondered if they realized how little and young he was and felt cautious, or if they found him annoying. They sniffed him from head to tail. They nosed him and rolled him. They pawed him. They refused to play with him—at first.

Emmett never had patience for puppies. He curled his lip or growled when they climbed all over him—and, of course, and maybe even because of it, puppies fluttered around him anyway. If we went somewhere with puppies, they found Emmett. I suppose his calm, solid presence helped them feel secure, or maybe they knew they could learn "to dog" from him as Lucas had done.

Scooter was no different. He clambered on Em. He yipped at Em.

Until Emmett taught Scooter his rules: *Don't drink when I'm drinking or I'll growl at you. Don't try to take my toys from me or I'll growl at you. Don't come near my food when I'm eating or I'll growl at you. Don't sniff me when I'm pottying or I'll growl at you.*

Scooter clocked in at a whopping six pounds, but he grew at an astonishing rate. Within a couple weeks, he lengthened to thin out some of that puppy fat. He ate voraciously. We had to open the pantry door quickly, step in, close the door, and scoop kibble into their bowls, because one second's hesitation and Scooter dove headfirst into the bag and started gobbling as fast as he could until we pulled him out.

When we adopted both Emmett and Lucas, they weren't babies. Emmett was at least a couple years old, and Lucas was close to a year. Both lived in shelters but somehow figured out house training almost immediately. Emmett's accidents occurred in the early days when he suffered from separation anxiety. Lucas never had accidents.

Scooter's house training threw us.

We took him outside after every meal, after playing, upon waking up in the morning, or upon waking up from a nap. He'd putter around outside, sniffing and exploring. When he went to the bathroom, we praised and rewarded him with a treat. Then we'd go back inside.

Exactly what we were supposed to do.

Except an ice storm hit. About a week into fostering Scooter, several inches of ice slammed our town and coated the grass in a thick layer of slick, slippery ice.

We bundled up, walked outside, lured him into the yard, and he ran straight back to the door. We picked him up and set him back in the yard. He ran straight to the door. He squeaked. He shivered. He cried. He begged to go in, to be picked up. After five minutes, we'd say, "Okay, we'll try again in a little while."

He'd sprint inside, dash into the living room, and squat on the rug.

We struggled between wanting his house training to be reliable and maintaining his safety in the below-zero temps and ice-covered backyard. I bought him a tiny coat to keep him warm while we worked on the house training, but he figured us out. He'd see us grab coats and put on boots, and he'd scamper off and poop under the TV before we could make him go outside.

By the time the ice melted, the pattern was set. He'd cry and whine and shiver and squeak each time we took him out, and he had no problem peeing in the house. It was warm there.

Around this time, we renamed him. He didn't seem like a Scooter, so we changed it: Scooter became Cooper. It fit him.

Cooper lived with us for four more weeks before we got a call from the rescue. Could we bring Cooper to an adoption event next weekend? He and his littermates were ready for their forever homes.

I muted the phone. "Can we drive Cooper to an adoption event this weekend? His litter is going up for adoption at the fairgrounds."

John gaped at me. His eyes widened. He scooped Cooper up into his arms. "No," he said. "No way."

I hit unmute. "Actually, can you please email us the adoption paperwork?"

That's where *my* dogs came from: two strays and one unplanned puppy. Two from shelters, one from a rescue. All three started life unwanted, unloved, uncared-for.

But how did they come to be in those situations to begin with? How did Emmett end up wandering the woods in Virginia while Lucas scrounged for food in trash cans in North Carolina? How did Cooper end up one of many puppies from unwanted litters, dumped for someone else to handle?

How did we humans end up with shelters crammed full of dogs when, moments ago—on an evolutionary scale, anyway—they ran wild and free?

After wolves and dogs diverged—molecular evidence suggests this divergence started 130,000 years ago—dogs became our partners. At the time, humans hadn't yet developed agriculture, so their camps moved around. Some researchers believe dogs realized humans could provide a warm place to sleep and scraps to eat, so the ones who looked the most in need of care—large eyes, for instance, like human babies—found their way into the homes and hearts of these nomadic people. The importance of "cuteness" to humans is evolutionarily beneficial for animals like dogs because we are instinctively drawn to protect and nurture babies. Dogs' adorableness and their neoteny—that is, retaining their juvenile features into adulthood—could be an evolutionary trick they played on us soft-hearted humans.

Other researchers stick to the mutually beneficial theory that dogs alerted humans to predators and helped them hunt, while humans provided safe spaces for dogs. Regardless, we've lived together, worked together, and eaten together for many thousands of years.

People began breeding dogs purposefully in the nineteenth century. Shortly thereafter, animal shelters popped up around the United States to deal with an overpopulation of stray and unwanted dogs. Most shelters aimed to house and find homes for these dogs rather than bludgeon or drown them, which had been the common practice. And while shelters have improved immensely and animal welfare laws attempt to prevent cruel deaths, the overpopulation of dogs persists.

It's not too difficult for unscrupulous folks to overbreed dogs for money. Puppy mills—mass breeding facilities known for inhumane treatment of their "stock"—proliferate because many honest people who really want a dog simply don't know about them. They buy a dog from the mall or an internet ad without a clue as to how the puppy or its parents were treated.

Lots of well-meaning people adopt from shelters, find dogs being rehomed online, or take a puppy from a friend whose dog had a litter—and later realize the dog doesn't fit their lifestyle. Or the dog doesn't behave in a particular way. Or the dog ages, gets sick, destroys the couch. And out the dog goes, packed off to an animal shelter.

It's a tricky set of problems because the shelter system, at least in the United States, needs to meet two very different kinds of needs. First, animal shelters need to care for homeless animals. This care can include everything from providing food and water to vaccinations and grooming, along with basic housing needs. This is an expensive business, and while some shelters are subsidized by the government, many rely on donations and adoption fees to cover their costs. The goal, of course, is to adopt out the animals as soon as possible after they come in to keep those costs low.

Cooper's adoption proved the rule. In fact, he never ended up in an animal shelter at all. He landed with a breed-specific rescue group who then placed him in foster care, where the costs can be much lower. Sure, the rescue would've covered his food and veterinary care, but no shelter needed space to house him or paid staff to take care of his needs. We took care of all that as his foster family.

Shelters like those that housed Emmett and Lucas purport to be no-kill, meaning they'll keep the animals in their care until they're adopted—or, sometimes, euthanized for a health concern or serious behavioral problem. Not all shelters can afford such a luxury.

Which leads to the second thing animal shelters need to do. Animal shelters serve to keep the public safe: safe from stray animal bites and safe from zoonotic diseases. Many county shelters are "open-admission" shelters, which means they are required to take in any animal that shows up—even, famously, a cow that was brought to a Brooklyn shelter, having escaped the slaughterhouse. The cow was later ushered into rescue at a farm sanctuary through the efforts of comedian Jon Stewart. County shelters, usually funded by taxpayers, are often required to take care of any animal that shows up or that poses a threat to the community.

These shelters are often derided as "kill shelters." I found myself swayed by the propaganda against this type of sheltering, and we consciously opted for two shelters marketed as "no-kill." I made a lot of assumptions about what a county shelter would be. In my imagination, it was an echoey, blocky building, probably with concrete walls separating the kennels and chain-link gates. I imagined it would be a smelly, noisy place full of chaos, staffed by an apathetic government worker who stamped adoption applications.

In hindsight, and with a lot more understanding, I now realize homeless animals in this country couldn't survive without both types of shelter—along with all sorts of rescues from breed-specific to size-specific to geography-specific. Many animals are housed in warm, inviting, comfortable shelters, and almost all types of animal shelters are staffed by kind, caring humans doing their best to help animals while fighting off debilitating compassion fatigue.

According to statistical data from the ASPCA, in the United States, estimates put the number of dogs in animal shelters at around 3.1 million. Slightly over two million of those dogs are adopted and almost 400,000 are euthanized. The remaining counts are chalked up to strays who are ultimately reunited with their owners. But of the 78 million dogs owned in the US, only 23 percent came from an animal shelter. Despite the sheltering system, a full 6 percent of owned dogs are dogs people found as strays.

Dogs came from wolves, wild and free.

Now they come from roadside farm stands, county pounds, a neighbors' unexpected litter, Nextdoor.com listings, breeders, large-scale rescues of hoarding situations and dog fighting rings, puppy mills via pet shops, strays, no-kill shelters, animal sanctuaries, craigslist...basically anywhere. And more puppies are born every day.

Spay and neuter initiatives decrease the number of dogs in shelters. Plus, with microchipping and rapid-response social media pages, lost dogs are likely to get reunited with their owners. Yet, dogs still face a homelessness crisis.

It's a baffling and complicated problem. We humans bred dogs to work for us. We bred them to serve as protectors, guardians, shepherds, and companions. We took the wild wolf and turned him into a fluffy friend. And yet, because dogs are so fully integrated into human society, we expect them to be almost human themselves. We expect our dogs not to growl, bite, sniff, bark, eat garbage, or run out the front door. We expect our dogs to stay in the yard, play nicely with every other dog they meet (even though none of us like every other human we meet), and eat dry kibble while ignoring the charcuterie board set out on the coffee table for your dinner guests. We expect our dogs to be friendly, unafraid, gentle, and still protective of our families. And when they fall short, we ditch them.

Among the reasons dogs are relinquished to shelters each year, behavior is an often-cited reason, as are financial issues and a lack of affordable pet-friendly housing. Initiatives all over the country are working to mitigate the impact of financial struggles by providing free pet food, discount vaccinations, and databases of affordable housing. There are practical solutions to those concrete problems if communities are willing to invest in them.

Behavior, though, is an interesting conundrum with a less specific solution. Studies conducted in 1999 and 2002 found dogs coming into shelters were more likely to have been housed outside or untrained by their families. Many of the behavior risks for relinquishment include barking, jumping up, and destroying things around the house. All of those can be mitigated, though training can be cost prohibitive. Some shelters around the country are offering free or low-cost behavior consultations because they've found a bit of training to keep the dog in the home is far more cost effective than bringing the dog back into the shelter for full-time care and feeding.

There's a direct link between normal dog behavior—like barking—and relinquishment.

Those behaviors, though, are only a human problem. And even then, it's only a problem for your dog if it's a problem for you. I don't mind if my dogs bark. I definitely don't mind it if I'm home alone with my two small children; their ferocious racket at the leaf blowing across the front porch makes me feel safe. But, I also know that if I wanted them to stop, I could teach them how to be quiet on cue—not dump them at an animal shelter.

Emmett's desire to eat everything in sight (or, rather, everything in *smell*) stemmed from starvation in his formative years. His behavior was costly, dangerous, and destructive. It was also manageable. But, perhaps with another adopter, it would've been a deal-breaker. Same for Lucas's fearful aggression and Cooper's soon-to-be-discovered unique brand of anxiety.

After we adopted Cooper, we filled his first year with puppy training class—clicker training class, socialization exercises, trips, hikes, anything to keep him happy and engaged while working on his behavior. He loved other dogs. He'd see one coming down the aisle in the pet store and get into a pounce position, tail up and wagging, ready to play. He nailed his clicker training class, so we enrolled him in a trick training class and booked some private sessions with the trainer. He thrived.

At least, he seemed to, minus typical little fears like umbrellas and vacuums. His startle reflex, too, seemed a little off. If someone came around the corner, or if he heard an unfamiliar sound, he bounced around barking his head off, fur standing on end, just like the other dogs—but it took him much, much longer to recover from those instances. I suspected something with his vision or hearing, but both checked out fine. He was just jumpy.

Otherwise, Cooper spent his puppyhood cuddling and playing, eating and sleeping. He seemed to be developing at a normal pace.

What happened next felt like I failed my sweet, friendly, happy puppy. It happened so gradually, it took a long time to fully understand the gravity of our situation, to grasp it was even happening in the first place. Despite his brilliance, despite our hard work, despite his solid foundation, something changed.

Things with Cooper were not right.

For most of my life, I believed many things about dogs—they are all friendly, they swim, they love playing with other dogs, they only see in black and white—some of which proved to be true. Others were way off. (Dogs, by the way, do see colors. They can see yellow and blue. And not all dogs can swim. Lucas could not.)

Yes, there are many traits that make a dog a dog. No matter where the dog comes from, if you unravel his DNA, you'll find a few, immutable characteristics.

In the beginning, there were wolves.

Then there was Emmett and Lucas and Cooper, and they showed me how wrong my assumptions were.

CHAPTER 3

Dogs with Character to Spare

When you sit quietly, when you struggle to speak up or to speak out, when you spend every class or meeting praying not to get called on, you get overlooked. And for most of my life, that was my goal: not to be seen.

Teachers, already spread too thin with too many students, ignored me. I did my work. I did it on time. I passed my tests. I simply never spoke. It was easier for teachers to ignore me because I wasn't having problems with the coursework, and I wasn't having problems with behavior, so why bother? The only classes I struggled in required speeches, participation points, or algebra.

A few teachers tried to crack me. My third-grade teacher sat me next to Patrick, the chattiest kid in class, probably in an attempt to stop him from talking so much; however, she ultimately delivered him a champion listener. My sixth-grade social studies teacher asked if I'd be willing to sit next to David, a hulking, aggressive boy who struggled with the material. The teacher thought I could pull David along and it would encourage me to speak more. Instead, David copied all my work, and I was too timid to say anything about it.

My eleventh-grade history teacher asked me to stand up in class each day and read a quote aloud. He told me I couldn't possibly succeed in college if I couldn't learn to speak in class.

One of my writing professors in grad school took another tactic. She asked me to stay after class and told me she thought I was rude, aloof, and disrespectful. "You don't even bother to contribute," she sneered. Her comment stung—not because her read on me was so wildly incorrect, but because I loved graduate school. I loved the hard work and the challenge, and I especially loved the workshops, even if I struggled to participate. I really did want to speak up and join the conversation. It was just impossible. Instead, I wrote detailed feedback for my classmates, but for that teacher, it wasn't enough. "You need to participate in the discussion or you will not pass," she threatened.

That year, a girl in my essay writing workshop wrote a piece about begging her parents for a dog when she was a high school junior. Her parents didn't want a dog, but she wore them down until they purchased her a Collie as pretty as Lassie. The essay unraveled the tale of this poor dog, the sole responsibility of a seventeen-year-old girl. She wrote about the hilarity of throwing a pool party when her parents were out of town and her friends getting the dog drunk on cheap beer. The year after buying the dog, the girl left for college, and her parents—who never wanted the dog to begin with—gave the Collie to someone else. The essay ended with the girl home for a visit from college, watching through her windshield from across the street as the dog played in the new family's yard. The concluding scene tried to portray the girl as a heroine—tearful, self-sacrificing, ignoring her own happiness for her dog's.

After her piece was workshopped, the professor asked if anyone had additional thoughts. His questions were pointed: Beyond the technical, does anyone want to comment on this piece? Any thoughts about the content? No one stirred. He waited.

I, who never spoke up in workshops for any reason, squirmed in my seat. I looked around the room and prayed someone else would jump in. Anyone. Anyone other than me. No one raised their hands.

Finally, I thought about Emmett and Lucas, took a deep breath, felt my face burn deep crimson, and said, "There's a problem with the tone." And then I threw up in my brain.

The professor nodded. "Explain."

"Well," I gulped. This was the first time I'd ever strung together more than two sentences in this class and I could feel the essay writer gaping at me from across the table. "This is essentially a story about a family ignoring a dog for a year and then giving her away, but the tone is supposed to seem lighthearted and funny when it's actually very sad."

My face flamed. The conversation continued from there for a minute or two, but I didn't hear any of it. I glanced up and saw the writer of the essay openly glaring at me. When it was her turn to respond, she defended her love for that dog while staring straight at me. I shrank as far as I could, attempting to become one with my chair.

I vowed never to speak in class again. I'd continue putting all my thoughts in the written notes and keep my mouth closed.

While I took writing classes at night, I worked a day job in an office a few blocks from campus. One Monday morning, a few minutes after our weekly staff meeting should have started, the agitated VP of our division barked, "We need to start meetings on time. Where's Maggie? Where's Alice?"

Alice was out sick. I sat in the first chair to his right.

"I'm here," I squeaked. He startled and gaped at me like I popped up through the floor.

I was young. I somewhat liked my job and the people I worked with, but I felt uncomfortable all the time. I sat in meetings unsure of what to say and when. I couldn't figure out how to break into a conversation with a new or different idea without stammering or losing my train of thought.

My lifelong struggle has been to feel comfortable taking up space, to feel comfortable using my voice. Every parent-teacher conference of my academic career sent my parents home with the same note, "She needs to participate in class more." My performance reviews at my first job and all the jobs that followed always included some version of, "Speak up more!"

I found ways around speaking out, appearing to participate more without *actually* participating more. I volunteered to take notes or to send a recap of the meeting with my ideas afterward. It made me seem involved, and I didn't have to open my mouth beyond a quick, "I'll do it," when someone asked for a volunteer notetaker.

Even after I changed jobs and spent several years in the pet industry, my reluctance to put myself out there, to be seen, plagued me. I remained invisible, comfortable, but also forgettable. One year, I attended the Global Pet Expo—an event I had been to many times before—and wandered the show floor with my friend and colleague, Carol. While we chatted, a woman ran over to hug Carol. They talked for several minutes while I hung to the side, until Carol asked her, "Do you know Maggie?"

"No," she said, shaking my hand. "We haven't met." Though we had met, of course, many times.

So often women learn to shrink. To take up as little space as possible. To be small. In meetings, women get dismissed or talked over or excluded altogether. We see it happening to others and cringe. We feel it happening to ourselves and discomfort settles like a rock. Our societal conditioning is tough to overcome. Combined with my social anxiety, my shyness, and my propensity to think instead of speak, it all meant I was forgettable. No one ever saw or heard me.

A dear friend and public relations professional told me I needed to figure it out. "You'll never get anywhere," she said, "until you can get yourself out there. Speak. Get on a morning show. Whatever. But unless you do something, you won't go anywhere."

Maybe I don't want to go anywhere.

I don't know what I was so afraid of back then. While I'm still not a big speaker-upper—unless it comes to animals and their treatment—that fear of censure is mostly gone. I take deep belly breaths to settle my body and prevent flushing, and I still turn red when I talk, but the terror I felt about having other people *look at me* disappeared. Now, when I give talks, people often ask me what changed.

Dogs. I adopted dogs who needed me to be their voice since they didn't have a voice of their own.

Public speaking still makes me nauseated. My stomach roils. I sweat. A lot. I plan my outfits around how much I sweat. I forget how to speak and breathe at the same time, so my words come out breathless or I have to pause to take deep, jagged breaths.

To learn to speak in front of others, I carefully scripted everything I planned to say. I even wrote out all the "casual asides" and where they'd go, when to pause, when to breathe. Still, I'm most comfortable silent. I prefer to sit on the edge, to watch, to listen. When I do speak, I crack jokes because, if people are laughing, they don't look at you too intensely. At business events and conferences, I hang by the bar. I stuff cheese and olives in my mouth to have something to do with my hands and hope for someone to come talk to me, to shield my awkwardness, even for a moment, from everyone else.

In the 2010s, introversion became a hot topic. There were books, TED Talks, seminars. I devoured them all, hoping to find a way to move more comfortably in the world. As a shy introvert, the world isn't a comfortable place for me. My house? Super comfortable. A loud, busy coffee shop where I can set up my laptop in a corner, put on my headphones, and write? Also super comfortable. The library? Heaven. Literally anywhere else? I feel itchy.

These personality traits probably make me more inclined to be an animal lover. Research shows introverts tend to be cat people, while extroverts tend to be dog people. It makes sense to an extent: Cats live at home, while dogs need to get out and about to, at a bare minimum, meet their daily bathroom requirements. Cats are quiet. Many dogs aren't. Cats tend to take good care of themselves, to be solitary and independent. Dogs, well…dogs need us to survive. Not that I would ever want our cats, Newt and Ripley, to get lost outside, but I'm confident they could keep themselves alive if they ever slipped out of the house. Cooper? He'd spend the whole time he was lost shivering and waiting for someone to come get him.

Studies have looked at multispecies homes and the personality traits of the dog-and-cat owners. Researchers found them to be somewhere on the spectrum closer to dogs, but more middling. That's me. Middling.

There's no shortage of methods for classifying and typifying people: the Myers-Briggs, the Enneagram, Winslow Personality Profile, ink blot tests. We can answer online quizzes that tell us what type of pizza we are, what *Friends* character we most resemble, and what dog breed we are. (Me: INFJ, 9w1, veggie pizza, Rachel, and Scottish Terrier.)

Dogs seem to have as much variation in personality as people do. Luckily for them, there are far fewer tests to classify and sort them into "types." Unfortunately, though, all those studies about people's pet preferences assume a significant degree of extroversion is universal to all dogs. But what about dogs who are naturally more introverted?

Emmett, the typical extrovert, thrived among people. He preferred lots of people paying lots of attention to him. He loved noisy, bustling situations. He pranced and preened when big crowds of kids jostled for his attention. He inserted himself into groups of people, and he ensured everyone in every group setting got a turn to pet him. He felt comfortable and happy situated among hordes of his admiring fans. A classic extrovert.

There's another stop on the extroverted-introverted spectrum: ambiversion. This trait sits not quite in the middle, but close. Depending on the person, the trait often skews slightly more one way or the other, but only by a smidge. Ambiverts are those people—and dogs—who identify as neither an introvert nor an extrovert but can see traits of both in themselves.

Lucas embodied ambiversion. It took lots of activity and play and snuggles and quiet moments and independent chewing time all together to fill his cup. Somehow he had the self-awareness to figure out when he needed to step away—a skill I'm still working on.

One Christmas, we drove with the dogs from DC to my parents' house in Indiana for a family dinner. Many of my extended family members—aunts, uncles, cousins, my great aunt—were coming, and we planned to stay a couple days to enjoy the festivities. Emmett, of course, ran from person to person requesting scratches and his share of the appetizers. Lucas wove in and out of the crowd until, suddenly, we realized he was gone.

"Where's Lucas?" I asked John. I thought maybe he let him outside or took him up to the guest room.

"I was going to ask you the same thing."

"Lucas!" I called. "Lucas, where are you?" I wandered around the house, gently calling his name until I walked into the living room.

Thump, thump, thump, thump.

"Lucas?"

Thump.

Cooper, though, might be the most like me—introverted and shy. In big groups, he moves to the edge of the room, even if he knows everyone there. He tends to pick one person (usually me) to stand by, and he never, ever relaxes in group settings.

Cooper has an advantage over introverted humans. When I'm in a big group setting, even if I'm incredibly uncomfortable, the expectation for us is to rise to the occasion. Extraversion among humans is, after all, the default. For Cooper, when he's uncomfortable and everyone sees his true self, most people feel nothing but sympathy and concern for him. As for John and I, we accommodate Cooper's discomfort. For him, his signs of overwhelm look like excessive barking, frantic dashing around, an inability to settle, and lots and lots of licking. We try to head it off before it gets to the anxiety stage. "Let's give Coop some space to recharge." Luckily for me, his ideal recharge is to curl up under the covers with me. Most of the time, though, it's removing him from a stressful situation so he can chill out in peace.

"Just be yourself," the extroverted among us extol. Myself? I would be home under the covers with Cooper, a glass of wine in one hand and a thick novel in the other. I would be in sweats, nestled under a weighted blanket with a pen and notebook, writing my thoughts, not speaking them. To get through a typical day, I need to be a slightly less authentic version of myself; I need to be a version of myself who cringes from discomfort on the inside but smiles with warm friendliness on the outside. At least, I *hope* that's what my smile says, because I probably am uncomfortable and don't want to look creepy to boot.

Meanwhile, Cooper can excuse himself; we give him a choice and strive to accommodate him. We put him in a quiet, safe space where he can settle. We plan gatherings at a restaurant or a park so he can stay home, where he's most himself. I'm jealous of his freedom, of his ability to be himself at all times, and to be accommodated because of who he is.

Appearing on the Knowledge at Wharton Podcast to talk about humans' need for quiet, introversion expert Susan Cain said, "...there are introverts and extroverts in almost every species of the animal kingdom, all the way down to fruit flies. You see fruit flies who tend to sit still in place and then other fruit flies who roam around in an exploratory way. That is true because these two types of different survival strategies exist in the animal world. But of course, the same thing is true with humans."

And, I would add, dogs.

Of course, change is always possible. Lucas came to us terrified. He feared so many things—people included—that had we given him a personality test then, it would've come back as shy, anxious, fearful, and unable to adapt.

But adapt he did.

It took years to dismantle the guard rails he'd constructed around himself. But once we did, it turned out he was silly, playful, mischievous, friendly, and energetic. And incredibly outgoing. We simply gave him the time and space he needed to come into his own. We supported him by managing his environment and enrolling him in courses and working at his pace. It impacted his life (and ours) tremendously to become a self-actualized pup.

When I step back and look through the lens of Lucas, I realize: We need to do that for ourselves. We need the time and space to find our way. We need our environment to comfort us, and we need to take courses or counseling or therapy—whatever opportunities or activities encourage growth—to guide us at our own pace. Sure, we can typify and classify ourselves in a million ways, but we need to extend the grace and patience we give our dogs so we can fully come into our own.

Lucas's true personality veered toward extroversion. "If he were a college student," John said, "he'd be the frat guy tossing a keg off the roof."

Oftentimes, Lucas acted like a jerk. He knew he was doing something bad, but he did it anyway, and he did it with a gleam in his eyes that I spotted in those first months together. As he grew more confident and his innate personality emerged, it was clear: Lucas wanted to party.

So he did. He played constantly. When Emmett and Cooper wouldn't play with him, he asked to be let out into the yard, and he'd throw a toy for himself. He dug up the garden. He learned tricks, he solved food puzzles, he pummeled his brothers and his best friend, our next-door-neighbor dog, Cady. He ran it out at doggy daycare once a week. Lucas had fun.

Until he didn't.

He would lunge and aggress, but as time progressed, those scary moments happened rarely and became so predictable we could largely prevent them.

I spent my entire life feeling shy. Shyness and introversion, I learned, are not the same thing. Watching my dogs struggle with their behavior and witnessing the changes they each went through, and seeing how different the results were despite the exact same training, made me realize something: Behavior is a choice, but personality is not.

My introversion, my nature, was simply me. I could learn to harness the strengths of my inborn personality. Meanwhile, shyness is more like a behavior, and like Lucas, I could overcome some of the more crippling aspects of that behavior. But it would take training: counterconditioning and desensitization of my fears. But if Lucas and Cooper could do it, so could I.

The dogs were already making those shifts within me, even though I couldn't yet see it. But I never would've spoken up in class if it weren't for my dogs pushing me to be a voice for the voiceless.

As I worked to find my voice, I also started to train Emmett for his therapy dog registration—something that would push me far outside my comfort zone while allowing Emmett to work where he was happiest: with lots of people pouring their attention onto him. Therapy dogs work alongside their person in settings like hospitals and schools. Unlike a service dog, a therapy dog isn't specially trained to perform specific tasks. Instead, a therapy dog serves more generally to improve people's lives by offering comfort and support. Friendly, outgoing, and solid, I knew Emmett would make the perfect therapy dog. He interacted easily with everyone he met. He would be a natural.

Far-ranging studies on the effects of therapy dogs have shown their benefit to children battling cancer, seniors feeling lonely in assisted-living facilities, school children learning to read, heart patients recovering from surgery, dementia patients, children on the autism spectrum, stressed-out college students, and more. Dentists' offices around the United States utilize therapy dogs to calm terrified children during dental procedures by having the trained dogs climb into the chair with the kids. Airports station therapy dogs around terminals where overwhelmed and frustrated passengers can pause for pets.

Em and I attended training classes held in the open space at a pet boarding and daycare facility. It smelled like dog and echoed with barks. People milled around chatting while I stood on my spot and tried to look friendly and open so someone would come talk to us. I'm terrible at walking up to a stranger and launching myself into a conversation. Most conversations I entered with strangers happened because Emmett walked over and demanded their attention. He didn't care who he knew and who he didn't; anyone with a hand to pet him was fair game.

The class started, and I was called upon to introduce myself and Emmett. Everyone else, it seemed, had been taking the class for a while and knew each other. Some had already passed their therapy dog tests and were practicing for a renewal with another dog.

I hadn't scripted an introduction, so I stammered our names and sat down. My heart raced, and I felt my face flame red. I started to pat Emmett and to comb my shaking fingers through the thick fur along his neck. While he looked exactly like a typical pit bull mix—a strong, stocky build with a brindle coat—the fur along the sides of his neck grew thicker and puffier than the short, soft coat that covered the rest of him. As I rubbed his neck, he turned his head to gaze up at my face. I relaxed. The irony felt sharp: I was on the receiving end of some therapy from the dog I was training to do therapy.

We began class in September and didn't take our test until May. Before showing up on our first night, I researched the therapy dog test and therapy dog work, but I was unclear on the training rigor. Emmett was trained, but he wasn't trained for therapy settings. While I knew he'd be great at therapy work, the training ended up being tougher for Emmett than I anticipated. While he was confident and outgoing, some of his Mr. Personality traits meant we had a lot of work to do. For instance, in a therapy setting, he wouldn't be able to shove his face into everyone's hands. Instead, he had to learn to wait to be invited.

The class also included exposure to medically specific distractions—like wheelchairs, walkers, and loud noises—while he responded to basic cues like heel, sit, and stay. One night in class, feeling tired and distracted, I dangled Emmett's leash from my finger. His heel seemed solid, but as we completed yet another circuit of the room, he suddenly sprang up and into the wheelchair. Whoever used it last forgot to engage the breaks, and the wheelchair shot across the room. Emmett leapt from it and sent the wheelchair flying. He waltzed back over to me, shook off, and sat. He looked up at me as if waiting for a treat. For a moment, the room was silent except for the sound of the wheelchair. It rolled across the room, bounced off the wall, and slowed to a stop in the center of the space. My mouth hung open while everyone burst out laughing.

"That's a good reminder to always lock the wheels on a wheelchair, you guys," the trainer said. "Emmett! What were you thinking?"

I can take a guess: He was tired. He saw a chair. He wanted to sit in it.

One night, as part of our training, we volunteered at a family event hosted by an elementary school. Our job was to talk about responsible pet ownership while the kids played with Emmett. He entertained dozens of kids, performed tricks, and allowed everyone to hug, high-five, or pet him. By the end of the night, he was wrecked, and so was I.

I packed up our things and dragged him to the door to leave. He wanted to stay on his mat and nap, not walk across the alley to our car. We stepped outside right as a teacher pulled up in her SUV. She popped the back gate open to load her supplies. As

Emmett and I walked around her car, he paused, then jumped into the back. Before I could respond, he laid down.

"Emmett, that's not our car!"

The teacher and her husband stopped with their arms loaded with boxes. They gaped at me wrestling Emmett out of their car.

Another therapy team walked out at that moment and laughed. "Did Emmett think that was your car?"

"No," I said. At the time I drove a tiny, four-door Saturn, not a giant SUV. "He probably thinks any car is good enough for a snooze and a ride home." I hefted him out of the SUV. I apologized profusely to the baffled car owners and raced toward my Saturn. I couldn't get us out of there fast enough.

Later, at home and settled, I relayed the story to John. "He jumped into someone else's car," I said. John laughed. It was so like Emmett to trust things to work out in his favor. He wanted a nap and a ride, and here's a car. Let's go!

Emmett and I soon started a weekly therapy program with the adolescent residents of a mental health facility. On a typical Friday, Emmett and I arrived at the hospital and sat in the lobby while we waited to be let into the rec room with the kids. Nearby, a woman ate a snack and watched Oprah on the small hospital TV. She kept glancing over at me and Emmett as I ran through some attentiveness drills with him. The receptionist paged the counselors we were meeting and said, "The therapy dog is here."

The woman looked over and smiled. "Oh, so he's a therapy dog!"

"He sure is," I said. "This is Emmett."

"He's very sweet," she said as he wagged his tail at her. He turned his soft brown eyes toward her face, imploring her for pets. She leaned down and scratched his ears.

"Does he know he's a therapy dog?" she asked.

I thought about it for a minute. Did he know what he was doing? "Honestly," I said, "I think he thinks I take him places to get petted."

Later, I considered the question a little bit more: What did Emmett think of his therapy work? Sometimes, especially with kids, he would gather up his gusto and become super energetic. He ran from child to child to get hugs and scratches. Other times, he responded to a situation in a way I could never train.

One Friday at the mental health facility, a young girl sat in the hallway crying. She was speaking with a counselor, and another one hovered nearby. The girl was distraught. The counselor sitting with her called over to us, "Can we say hi to your dog?"

I walked Emmett over, assuming he'd do his usual: plow into her, tail wagging, and smoosh himself into the young girl. Instead, Emmett moved purposefully toward her face. He gave her cheek a gentle sniff, then he laid against her thighs and placed his head in her lap. The girl smiled and cooed at him. Her tears stopped flowing as she rubbed Emmett's head. He gazed into her eyes calmly and thumped his tail lightly against the floor.

No matter how good a dog Emmett was at each and every visit, I could never teach him to respond perfectly in such specific situations. It wasn't trainable behavior. But somehow he always toned down or dialed up his exuberance to meet the patients' needs.

I spent most of my life not wanting to use my voice, to open my mouth, or draw attention to myself. I sat in back rows. I put my head down, did my work, and went home. But the more Emmett and I worked in public spaces and spoke with folks, the more I realized I needed to find my voice. Emmett and all those other animals couldn't speak for themselves. I wanted to speak for them.

After Emmett started work as a therapy dog, small bits of my fear of people, of speaking, disappeared. Like the training and counterconditioning I was doing with Lucas, with more repetitions, I felt more confident. People were so ecstatic to see Emmett and engage with him that it showered me with positive reinforcement to keep at it. I still had a lot of work to do, though. We both did.

"Why spend so much time/energy/money to help animals when people need so much help?"

"It's just a dog. What about abused kids?"

"I'm disappointed in people who care more for pets than for people."

Countless times I've heard similar complaints. Why devote resources to helping animals when people so desperately need help?

My response is, love isn't a finite resource. We can and should care about both. We need to care about both. Caring for animals and working for their well-being doesn't diminish our capacity to care for people.

Most of us don't have unlimited resources. What we all have, though, is the capacity to care. To be compassionate.

I never experienced a ton-of-bricks moment. It was never, "Ohhhhh, I get it. I need to be Emmett's voice." Instead, a series of small, individual conversations and singular incidents forced me to open my mouth and start talking.

There was the woman in our training class. "He's so sweet." Long awkward pause. "Will you put him down when you have kids?"

There was the woman in the lobby of the animal hospital too terrified to sit near Emmett, so she stood against the wall. "Isn't he aggressive?"

There was the carpenter we hired to repair our kitchen cabinets who refused to come in the house until I put Emmett in another room.

There were the movers helping us relocate who took one look at him and said, "He looks like he'd rip your face off."

Each time I heard a disparaging comment about him, my voice grew a decibel or two. After a few deep breaths, I gently explained, "His appearance and breed don't matter. People look different from each other, and we know it's wrong to judge anyone by how they look. Same for dogs. He's friendly. He loves people and tacos. His fur is bunny-rabbit soft. You're welcome to pet him."

I answered every question asked of us—has he ever bitten anyone (no), does he attack dogs (no), can he be around children (yes), are you afraid he'll turn on you (only to snitch a sandwich out of my hand, and even then I always share my lunch with him anyway)—with the kindest, most compassionate voice I could leverage.

Which was sometimes neither kind nor compassionate.

Like the time a friend-of-a-friend's wife stuck out her leg and put her foot into Emmett's chest. "Do not kick my dog," I growled. She huffed about how much she disliked big dogs and stomped off.

When the vet tech kept missing his vein for a blood draw, I opened my mouth. "Is there someone else who can help?" I relayed that experience with mighty indignation to my parents, and my mom laughed at me. "You never once asked for someone else to stick an IV in you, no matter how many times they missed," she said. "For Emmett? You'll do anything!"

It's the ultimate expression of the human-animal bond: being a voice for the voiceless. It takes a lot to be an effective and honest voice. I needed to learn about dogs in general, and my dogs in particular. I needed to understand how to advocate for them, and for dogs like them, in ways that might be successful in creating change instead of alienating people whose heels were already dug in.

What compelled me to train Em to visit with people? We drove to events where I needed to speak, and I took Tums and deep breaths. I tried to calm my nerves. My clammy hands gripped Emmett's leash as we walked into buildings and classrooms and hospitals. He pranced alongside me, head high, tail wagging, ready to greet his adoring fans.

When Emmett started working with kids and adult groups, I often stood in front of a classroom full of students and teachers with my stomach in a knot. I'd feel the heat rising into my face as I spoke about him and his work. It felt easier to talk about him than it ever was to jump into the fray of a meeting, but I still felt unsettled when I opened my mouth.

I continued my informal speaker training—my counterconditioning and desensitization—with each visit Emmett and I did together. Then the skills started to trickle over into the training I was doing with Lucas.

Lucas and I enrolled together in a course called "Reactive Dog I" at a local facility that came highly recommended. The first class session was people only, no dogs. I drove to class rehearsing my intro: "Hi, my name is Maggie. My dog is Lucas. He's an eighty-pound Shepherd mix who is reactive to all sorts of things, but mostly strangers, bikes, and other dogs. After years of work, he's finally over his fear of plastic bags, so I'm confident this class will help us with the others." Over and over, I repeated it on the drive to the training center.

Despite all the positive interactions and rehearsals I had accumulated through Emmett, public speaking—I discovered through Lucas—wasn't about giving speeches. It was all the little interactions throughout the day. I realized his advocacy required more than I felt comfortable with.

"We need space!" I shouted to people walking right up to him at the park.

"Get your dog!" I yelled to the guy down the path who let his off-leash dog barrel towards Lucas. "Don't worry!" the person often called back. "He's friendly!"

My dog is scared and reactive and your off-leash dog will probably provoke him into snarling and lunging, making him look mean and scary when he's really just terrified, so get your damn dog before my dog loses it. We are trying our best here!

Of course, I couldn't yell all that in the amount of time I had to keep a fight from happening, so I'd simply scream back, "My dog isn't!" The angry owner would snatch their dog away while glaring at me and Lucas.

During our reactive dog class, Lucas performed as requested. He walked when he was supposed to walk. He sat when he was supposed to sit. He whined the entire time—the trainer started calling him "whiny face"—but he did all the exercises without fail. In fact, he performed perfectly, which was a huge problem.

I needed to talk to the trainer.

I wrote out my key points in the draft of an email so I could look at it and hone it before our meeting. As much as I wanted to let it go and just keep working through class, I knew it wasn't serving Lucas; for as expensive as the lessons were, we needed to see progress.

I memorized my talking points and scheduled a meeting.

"Lucas knows we're training," I told the trainer. "He's done enough of this over the years and he's a brilliant dog. He knows these aren't real-life scenarios, so he isn't reacting. He isn't being himself because he's not scared. He's being, well…he's being *good*." He wasn't learning anything. I wasn't learning anything. We needed a bigger challenge.

She dismissed my concerns. Practice is what matters, she said. Repetition. Doing it over and over. She recommended we enroll in the next level, Reactive Dog II, which included more real-life scenarios because the class was held outdoors instead of in the training center.

I filled out the enrollment form and drove us home, stopping for a puppy latte for Lucas and a chai for myself. *We both deserve a treat*, I thought. Lucas for his work in class and me for speaking to the trainer about my concerns instead of complaining to John at home until the course ended. I only wished she hadn't dismissed us so handily.

In between sessions of Lucas's reactive dog course, I continued to train with Emmett and to work in animal-assisted activities with him. The dichotomy between the two dogs challenged me, not only as their advocate, but as their trainer. It stretched me and made me work harder than I would have if they had been similar to one another. They were opposing forces, and training two different dogs with such different behaviors kept me on my toes.

Through the therapy dog organization, the Delta Society (now called Pet Partners), Emmett and I were invited to speak to health organizations and to schools about the power of animal-assisted therapy. We attended a session with our state representative to speak about Emmett's work with the adolescent residents of the mental health facility. She spent as much time scratching Emmett's head as she did asking questions about the program. We appeared in articles profiling "hero" dogs who help children. We visited so many schools and libraries in our town, kids started to recognize Em when we were out and about.

As Emmett rose to fame, I kept my hand steady on his back. The irony was not lost on me: I stood in front of groups talking about how dogs can bring confidence and self-assuredness to children, about how dogs can help calm anxieties, about how dogs can encourage children to try something challenging with a furry friend by their side; all the while I wove my fingers into his fur to keep myself grounded, to soak up a bit of his comfort.

If only that could've worked for Lucas, too.

CHAPTER 4

More than Friends: Dogs as Family

I stepped into the community room at the fire station with Emmett by my side. I took a deep breath, my right hand white-knuckling his green nylon leash.

We can do this. We can do this. We can do this. I hope you can hear my thoughts. Emmett, we can do this.

The therapy dog exam consisted of a series of cues and challenges that tested basic manners, like walking nicely on a leash and accepting gentle pats, alongside real-world scenarios, like a restraining hug or angry yelling. I knew Emmett would pass all but two scenarios, and those two—ignoring an approaching dog and not taking food offered by a stranger—were so questionable in my mind that my heart thudded and I kept sending silent messages to Em: *We can do this.*

Aside from dog food, dog training might be the most controversial topic in pet care.

The controversy stems from how humans regard our animal friends. Many people, even many pet professionals, think of nonhuman animals as lesser. Their mindset is, we are at the top of the food chain, the evolutionary end point, so we are better than the animals. We think and feel, and they don't.

So the argument goes.

You are its master, someone wrote in the comments on a blog post I wrote about not minding that the dogs sometimes tug on their leash when we walk together. *It should do what you ask.*

My dogs are my partners. Lucas, he—not *it*—does what I ask because we love to work together, and I would never ask him to do anything to compromise our trust. I worked too hard for too many years to put our bond at risk. Same for Emmett and Cooper. Plus, I don't consider myself the master of anyone. Not another person, not another animal. Why, I wonder, would I even want to be when I'm barely master of myself?

The master mentality has allowed people to use force and pain when working with dogs. They use pronouns like "it" instead of "he" or "she," which gives the illusion that dogs are a *what* instead of a *who*. These types of trainers focus on dominating and subduing. And this continues despite mountains of evidence published in scholarly journals about the depth of our dogs' abilities to think, to reason, to feel.

"Master" is an arrogant term. I want to work together with my dogs because we're a team, not because they're afraid I'll hit, shock, or choke them. Even if science weren't shining a bright light down the path of change, doesn't it feel like a more humane approach to training? A kinder way of working together than dominance and mastery?

On the flip side of all this controversy sits your average dog owner. Most dog owners—or pet parents—don't have the depth of knowledge about the skirmishes waged on the dog training battleground. Most dog owners simply go about life with their dogs, teaching them what they need to, sometimes with the help of a trainer readily available at a national pet store chain. If you ask any of those dog owners to talk about the theories or science behind how they interact with their dogs, my guess is most wouldn't have read the data but would clearly state: My dog is my best friend. My dog is more than just a dog. My dog is a member of our family.

We are at a unique place in human history: We have a deep understanding of the animals who share this planet with us, and our knowledge is firmly rooted in science. It's rich. It's full of nuance and specificity. Best of all, this understanding is based on research and data, rather than a religious or agricultural or cultural interpretation.

Major universities around the globe—like Duke, Yale, and Eötvös Loránd University in Hungary—boast canine cognition labs and publish groundbreaking papers. Experts conduct functional magnetic resonance imaging (fMRI) on our dogs to show us how their brains operate in real time. Researchers gather chemical data from saliva and urine. Scientists capture pictures of dogs' brains when they see, smell, and hear.

In one example, researchers studied almost 1,000 dogs whose owners said their dogs showed signs of aggression. They took a look at each dog's medical history to identify any underlying condition that might cause the behavior. Researchers found about 15 percent of the dogs' medical conditions contributed to their aggression. Once medical causes were ruled out, the researchers delved into the training methods the owners used with their dogs. They found punitive training methods—like using electronic shock collars—correlated to negative improvement. In other words, those dogs' aggression worsened. Dogs who were trained with systematic desensitization and counter-conditioning—like what we used for Lucas—improved.

With more and more studies like this one, data piles up. Behaviorists and veterinarians interpret the research, teach owners, and change our approach to animal training. Right?

Well, not exactly.

If you glance through the comments on any article about the evolution of dog training methods, many comments boiled down to, "Nuh uh." Even articles that detail the science behind a behavioral approach—one both humane and effective because it's based on peer-reviewed scientific research—receive scornful comments and derision. Or commenters use elaborate anecdotal evidence about their own dogs who they trained entirely by collar yanks or electronic shocks, and how they're the very best of friends. So, clearly, science is wrong.

But the research shows, over and over again, that these outdated training methods are to the detriment of our dogs, as well as our relationship with our dogs.

And I want a good relationship with my dogs.

Many of the people who leave these comments on articles and blogs seem, to me, to ignore a key component of communication: It's a two-way street. Demanding your dog perform a specific behavior isn't the same as communicating with your dog. If your dog understands what you're asking—and maybe even *why* you're asking it—he might be more inclined to respond, to work *with* you instead of *for* you. Likewise, if you're open to two-way communication with your dog, and you ask him to sit, he might indicate in some way—a shift of his haunches, a shuffle of his back feet—to tell you something like, "Hey, I'm a little sore today. Can I skip sitting for now?"

Dogs are exceptional communicators.

If only we'd listen.

The weekend after we adopted Emmett, we attended our first obedience class together and paired hand signals with verbal cues. In fact, Je'ree, my best friend and professional dog trainer, had us teach the hand signal before we taught the word cue. It worked. The hand cues worked perfectly whether we included the verbal cues or not.

An open palm asked Emmett to sit. A finger pointed to the ground asked him to lie down. A flat palm facing forward asked him to stay. Some gestures required a movement that mimicked the action. For instance, I twirled my pointer finger to ask him to spin in a circle. Other gestures seemed arbitrary, like when I raised my arm and made a fist to ask him to come to us.

Later, when I trained Emmett for the therapy dog exam, I used the same skills and the same research. I trained him with hand signals and positive reinforcement. And, though I felt anxious about the test, while I silently repeated to myself, *"We can do this,"* deep down, I knew we would pass—and we did. Although, in full disclosure, the only reason we passed the portion of the test when he needed to ignore a neutral dog who was supposed to be ignoring him, *the neutral dog* actually stepped in front of the handler to greet Emmett. The handler was aghast, and the assessor let us repeat the exercise, but by then, Emmett had already "met" the dog and sailed right past. Phew.

Over the years, I enrolled in more hours of training courses than I could possibly count: basic manners, basic obedience, Canine Good Citizen, trick training, therapy dog training, Reactive

Dog I, Reactive Dog II, agility, group classes, workshops, one-on-one sessions with at least seven different trainers, and other classes that are more hazy in my memory. Most of the class time and most of the work established a stronger relationship between me and my dogs. We learned to read each other's subtle cues and to work together. In most cases, all the training we did served us positively.

In *most* cases.

A few trainers and their methods defied logic. We had a trainer suggest we throw water balloons at Lucas's feet when he lunged at another dog. Setting aside the logistics of actually filling and toting water balloons on our daily walks through the park, I couldn't figure out what splashing him with water would actually accomplish—other than bringing home a soggy dog several times a day. I suppose the goal was to startle him out of the reaction, but how was he learning anything? John and I quickly agreed: the water-balloon trainer wasn't for us. Or anyone else, for that matter.

Lots of trainers recommended punitive methods: If he lunges at another dog, pinch him with a choke collar or utilize an e-collar. This is the fancy way of saying give your dog electrical shocks. But how does hurting someone help them be less fearful? Imagine a small child calling for help because he's afraid there's a monster in his closet, and his caregiver pinches the skin on his neck to eliminate the fear. It made no sense to us.

Another trainer recommended feeding a reactive dog only when in view of triggers. Sort of like a counterconditioning protocol on steroids. The idea was to shift his mindset from "scary thing I must react to in a violent way to keep myself safe" to something like "this thing brings me yummy food, so it can't possibly be scary."

So, for Lucas, her idea was for me to take him and his food bowls out to the front porch and set it down for him to eat only when a bike or person or stroller or dog went past. He could eat when the trigger was present, then I was supposed to pick up his bowls and wait until the next obstacle went past. You can't possibly guarantee a stroller/bike/trash truck will go past your front stoop at mealtimes, so I wondered: Would we sit out there all night or all morning waiting?

I tried this method with his dinner once, and it was an unmitigated disaster. He barked and strained and lunged so much when the first dog went past, he knocked over his entire dinner bowl. After I refilled it to try again, we waited and waited and waited for someone to pass by the house. Fifteen minutes later, I knew we'd never get anywhere with the meals-on-the-porch method. I took him inside to eat his dinner in peace.

If we treated our friends the same way some dog trainers expect us to treat our dogs, we wouldn't have many friends. We know dogs have rich, complicated emotional lives and an incredible capacity for thinking and feeling. Why do some trainers think it's okay to push, prod, shock, pinch, roll, and yank our dogs?

Dogs are hardwired for communicating with humans. In a 2017 study, researchers showed dogs look at our faces, specifically our eyes, for cues. The researchers used eye-tracking technology and found dogs read your facial expressions first by scanning your eyes, then the rest of your face, and react accordingly. No other animals outside of humans, monkeys, and apes have been observed reading the face of another species before this study.

Other research has shown that dogs react positively to our voices and follow our gestures. Almost no other animal follows gestures, let alone gestures from another species. Our dogs follow our gestures, and they do it incredibly well. That's why working dogs can be fields away and still respond to hand cues from a great distance. They're genetically coded to watch us. Pet dogs don't need the repertoire of signals and cues a herding dog does, but because they evolved from watching us and respond better to visual cues than verbal ones—they don't, after all, have a capacity for spoken language—training with hand signals makes sense from a biological perspective.

I saw this play out with Emmett over and over again. When we worked with our group of residential kids at the mental health facility, they'd often "train" him to do something I had already trained. I didn't want the kids to fail, so for behaviors we had already worked on, I trained Em using the hand signals instead of the words well in advance of our sessions with the kids. While the kids leapt around and waved their arms and sang, "Spin, Emmett! Spin in circles! You can do it! Spin!" I stood behind them and circled my finger in the "spin" cue I already taught him. He spun. The kids cheered. Emmett strutted around, proud of making all those kids fawn all over him.

Nearing his thirteenth birthday, Emmett experienced hearing loss typical with a geriatric dog. Sometimes we'd walk into a room where he was chewing on a bone, and several minutes would pass before he looked up with a startled expression, followed by a happy wag that seemed to say: "Oh, hey! Glad you're home!" We never lost the ability to communicate with him, despite his diminished hearing. Instead, we focused on our hand signals and visual cues—like flickering the outside lights to call him in at night.

Hand signals work because they capitalize on our dogs' ability to watch us; that said, training with hand signals doesn't solve everything. My friend rescues and fosters deaf dogs, and in his house—with two deaf dogs and two hearing dogs—the deaf dogs always cause mischief the second he walks out of the room. They check the table and counters for food, get in the trash, and are generally naughty. But maybe, he said, it could be the hearing dogs who make all the mischief. When everything crashes off the counter or the trash clatters to the ground, the deaf dogs are happily enjoying the spoils while the hearing dogs, the ones who startled at the crashing noises, take off at a run before their owner gets back.

Ever since our first training class with Emmett, John and I trained all our dogs—and all the dogs who passed through our care—with hand signals. We realized they picked up the visual cues faster than the words, so why not use their genetic predisposition to our advantage?

When our daughter, Astrid, was born, she spent nine days in the NICU, and during her hospital stay, she failed her newborn hearing screen. They referred us to a pediatric audiologist who could see her several months later. At her first appointment, we discovered Astrid has mild-to-moderate hearing loss in both ears. Her official diagnosis is bilateral sensorineural hearing loss.

Leaving the appointment, I carried her out to the car, buckled her into her car seat, climbed in behind the wheel, and cried. They provided me with a diagram of what she was hearing. She couldn't hear birds chirping, she couldn't hear her older sister, Violet, singing to her, she couldn't hear me whisper "I love you" as I tucked her in at night. All the unknowns spread out before us frightened me.

Her doctor scheduled a follow-up screening to refine our understanding of what she could hear—it's tough to know for sure in an infant since she couldn't tell us anything. Between the two appointments, I researched everything I could about hearing loss in children. We connected with our state's health department, which provides an impressive number of early intervention services for kids with any degree of developmental challenges, and they started aligning support services for us, one of which was an American Sign Language teacher, Claire, who swooped in and literally saved the day for us and for Astrid. At our very first meeting, Claire helped our family figure out our next steps to support Astrid and to support our language learning.

Astrid eventually got hearing aids, but even with the hearing aids, we knew we needed to learn ASL as a family because, for one thing, she wouldn't be able to wear them all the time. They can't get wet. So, what do you do during bath time or pool time in the summer? What if she loses one and we have to wait for a replacement? What if the batteries die while she's at school or the aids malfunction? Or, since we don't know the cause of her hearing loss, what if it's degenerative and she eventually becomes profoundly deaf?

So we decided to learn a new language together. We started classes with Claire a few months after Astrid's diagnosis, and Violet picked up on signs immediately. As John and I practiced and practiced, we realized all of Cooper's hand signals were made-up gestures. The gestures didn't align with any ASL signs. We wanted to make a shift in our training to give us all the same foundation and to allow Astrid to communicate directly with Coop as she grew. It made perfect sense: We would transition his hand signals from the arbitrary obedience cues to American Sign Language signs.

One summer day, nine-month-old Astrid crawled around the living room floor, gumming toys, drooling everywhere, giggling, and playing. It was beautiful outside, so plenty of people were taking nice, long walks with their dogs. Cooper perched on the back of the living room sofa. When a dog passed by the front of our house, Coop went into his usual routine: raising his hackles, launching into a barking frenzy, and leaping from the back of the sofa to the armchair to the sofa to the armchair. In his little doggy brain, he seemed to think this routine kept our family safe from attack for the last ten years. In his head, his success rate was 100 percent perfect. We had never been attacked, after all—not by passing dogs, letter carriers, or Boy Scouts pulling tubs of popcorn in little red wagons.

That morning, while he leapt around the room barking his head off, I watched Astrid's little fingers come together and form the ASL sign for dog. It looks like snapping your fingers to call a dog to you, and her tiny little fingers formed the shape right in front of my eyes. I added my squeals and cheers to the cacophony of Cooper's barks, then I whipped out my phone and filmed the moment. Once Cooper calmed down, I wondered how long it would take for the reverse to happen. How long until Cooper responded to Astrid calling him with her sign?

Luckily, dogs are attuned to what we humans, even the littlest among us, do.

Ethologist and dog expert Ádám Miklósi wrote in a 2009 paper, as far as communication with humans goes, "...dogs have evolved certain skills that enrich their capacities to communicate with humans. This process started probably 20–25 thousand years ago, and passed over different stages." He goes on to say the fossil record bears out the special partnership between dogs and humans. We've even been buried with our dogs for the past ten to fifteen thousand years.

Dogs became dogs in part because evolution selected for dispositions that helped them understand us.

Our dogs understand us so well, in fact, that studies show they can tell when we're paying attention to them—and when we aren't. Other research demonstrates dogs can tell if we're talking to them or to someone else nearby, and they ignore known verbal commands if the speaker is looking at another human instead of at them while saying the cue word. Dogs can "read" human cues like pointing and gazing, too, and they do it better than wolves or apes. All these communication skills come from living alongside us for more than tens of thousands of years.

This ability for two-way communication works to make our bond with dogs even stronger. Dogs might be the only animals who can understand our social cues. How lucky are we to have an entirely different species with which to share our lives, our thoughts, and our feelings?

Of course, this ability to communicate enables us to work together with our dogs in all sorts of ways. We're able to train our dogs to be our helpers in purposeful ways, as with service dogs or shepherds, and we're able to train them to coexist with us in our homes as pets. Their evolutionary propensity to communicate with us makes this not only possible but fun. Still, even with our deep friendship, dogs are not humans and need to learn to exist with us safely.

When it comes to pet dogs, trainers and owners want an obedient dog. It makes sense: Not only do we not want anything bad to happen to our dogs, like running into a road or eating something toxic, dogs are also liabilities for us if something like a bite were to happen. So, we train our dogs. We teach them how to have manners to live successfully among humans. We use verbal cues, hand signals, scent markers, and more. We teach them—or, at least, we *try* to teach them—not to eat garbage, to come when called, to sit at the door and wait instead of barreling out after the UPS guy, to bark when there's danger but to stop barking if the phone rings. We teach them to sit nicely for their bowls of food, to stay off the sofa, and not to jump on Aunt Betty. Basic manners and cues—come, sit, shake, go get Mommy a beer—take time to build incrementally, but it's usually an uncomplicated process.

Evolution designed our dogs to work within our parameters, which makes training possible and, often, simple. But what happens when our dogs' lived experience fights against evolution?

Cooper came from a backyard breeder. The people who owned his mom dropped a litter of puppies at a vaccination clinic and essentially said, "Here's the litter. Take them." They had wanted to breed their dog with a pure pit, but when their dog got out of the yard and came back pregnant, her puppies were mixed. While we don't know anything about the dog who fathered Cooper's litter, we know the mama dog wasn't a "sound" dog. Soundness describes the overall health of dogs. According to the *Merck Veterinary Manual*, soundness is as follows:

> Breeding soundness means a dog or cat is free from heritable defects based on phenotype evaluations such as radiography (eg, elbow dysplasia), ultrasonography (eg, renal dysplasia, tricuspid dysplasia), ophthalmoscopy (eg, cataract), physical examination (eg, patellar

luxation) or specific DNA testing when available (eg, progressive rod-cone degeneration).

Obviously, unscrupulous backyard breeders conduct none of those careful tests.

Cooper came from wonky stock. Unsound. His biological foundation made his training that much harder. His brain worked against his biology. Training Cooper became less about obedience cues—the smart little cookie mastered those on the first try—and more about mitigating and managing his incredibly high anxiety.

Years before Cooper came along, we had the opportunity to learn how to work through fear with Lucas. But fear and anxiety are different beasts.

Lucas was most likely born on the street. A family in North Carolina found him rooting through their trash can, alone and only a few months old, on Thanksgiving Day. He'd been hit by a car and had a significant limp. His skinny frame was covered in mange and fleas. His rescuers took him to an animal shelter where he was slated for transport to Washington, DC.

By the time we adopted him the following April, nearly his entire first year of life consisted only of living on the streets and living in an animal shelter. He had no real-world experience beyond fighting for survival. He spent months living with both acute and chronic fear.

All we could do as his partners and allies in life was to let Lucas unravel on his own. He needed to lose the hair-trigger protective coating he'd built up around himself. We gave him space to escape: his favorite spot was in the corner of the living room behind an armchair. We gave him good food and plenty of exercise. We gave him opportunities to run and walk and sniff and play with Emmett.

I've always scrambled to find more hours in the day, to fit more in, to do more. Until Lucas, I never thought there was enough time in a day or a week or a month. I never thought I could pack in enough productivity into the hours I did have.

Then came Lucas. And Lucas demanded slow.

He needed generosity. He needed patience. He needed grace—especially when he made mistakes. He needed me and John to trust his tightness would unravel if we gave him some space. He hadn't yet figured out how to communicate with us, nor we with him. The two-way communication coded into his DNA was shrouded by a distrust so thick he would hardly look at us.

We enrolled in training classes, and in the meantime, I tried to find ways to help him around the house. His fear often made him act like a jerk, and I had to figure out how to manage his behavior to keep him—and those around him—safe, while allowing him the grace and freedom to dismantle his fear. And he was afraid of *everything*.

He hid when I turned on the TV.

He tucked his tail and cowered when John shook out a plastic trash bag.

He snapped and growled at any dog who came within spitting distance.

He tried to bolt if he saw something with wheels—a stroller, a bicycle, a little red wagon—coming toward us in the park.

Unlike Cooper, though, his genetics seemed to be sound. His body healed. As his fear fell away, I saw glimpses of his silly side. He immediately engaged in mischief the moment he felt a tiny bit braver. One night, John and I sat in bed reading. From the living room, we heard a *scritch-scritch-scritch*. I looked through the door, and there was Lucas, happily gnawing away at the wooden arm of our living room chair.

"What do you think you're doing?" I asked.

He wagged.

Another day, he watched Emmett chomp away on an antler, one of the most preferred dog chews in our house. I purchased one for each dog from a woman in Wyoming who collected naturally shed antlers, sawed them into pieces, and sold them as dog chews. Lucas had his own antler on his bed on the other side of the room, but he seemed entranced by Emmett's. A moment later, Lucas turned toward our front door, stood up from his bed, and woofed. Emmett jumped up from his bed and dashed to the door, barking to back up Lucas. But Lucas turned the other way and scampered over to Emmett's antler, picked it up, and carried it back to his bed. By the time Emmett realized there wasn't anyone at the door and returned to his chew, Lucas was settled on his bed, the antler held between his two front paws.

I retrieved Lucas's discarded antler to give to Emmett. "You naughty boy," I laughed as I patted Lucas's head. He wagged. We were getting there. We were starting to communicate. We could see how clever he was under that cloak of fear.

Our bond with our dogs is one of the few, if not the only, relationship in our lives free from judgment. Even if you're working together on a problem behavior, the trust between a dog and his or her family is vitally important. Consider Lucas and his lunging: The reality is he never wavered in his steadfast commitment to the family after he realized we weren't scary. If I had hurt him, if I had pinched him, if I had pushed him to the ground and held him there, I can't even fathom how much damage that would've done to the trust we worked so hard to build.

Even subjecting an easygoing, laid-back, unflappable guy like Emmett—who probably could've been more resilient—to a physical, punitive approach would not be worth the cost.

It's a relief that science is digging into the complicated mental lives of our companion animals, because it's much harder to justify using fear, intimidation, and force to get our dogs to do something when you know how much they think and feel. It's much preferred, then, to put in the time and effort to learn how to communicate with our dogs, how to work together and preserve the incredible gift that is our bond with dogs. We have the data and science to back up the call for better training methods.

These days, humanity's friendship with our dogs isn't based on survival. Most of us don't keep them around to scare off predators; that's probably why many dogs turn their tens of thousands of years of evolution on the UPS guy instead of a saber-toothed tiger.

While they might not protect us from being eaten, dogs do help us survive. Dogs lessen their people's worries, make them feel safer, and help them live a longer, healthier life. Meanwhile, people nurture their dogs, keep them safe, and help them stay healthy. It's still a symbiotic relationship. Only the parameters have changed.

In a 2018 study published in *Anthrozoös* that considered how dog owners shared their feelings with their dogs—versus what they told their confidants or partners, and compared to non-dog owners—researchers found something surprising to no dog lover: "For dog owners, their dog appeared to play a similar role as their partner, with greater willingness to talk to their dog about depression, jealousy, anxiety, calmness, apathy, and fear-related emotions, compared with a confidant."

We are lucky. Our dogs make us happy and keep us healthy. It's a fact; they keep us physically well. The American Heart Association (AHA) found people lowered their risk of heart disease when they acquired a pet. People who have heart disease and who own a pet are also more likely to survive a heart attack.

According to a 2014 Health & Science piece by Christie Aschwanden in the *Washington Post*, "One recent review of sixty-nine studies found evidence that human-animal interactions could lift mood and reduce stress and anxiety, perhaps by activating the hormone oxytocin."

The same article also reported survey results from the University of Utah: "Pet owners were less obese, had better self-reported health, less asthma and fewer cardiovascular problems than people without pets."

Having a dog keeps us healthy, but having our little furballs curled up at our feet is so much more. It's about heart health—not the cardiovascular kind the AHA is talking about—but our need for emotional wellbeing. It sounds sappy, but it's rooted in science. Caring for a pet lowers stress, alleviates depression, and eases anxiety.

Our dogs are our partners in health and wellness because, the article reported, "…pets can contribute to their owner's health by providing social support and daily exercise resulting in stress-reduction and improved immune system function, but they found a reduction in doctor visits only in long-term pet ownership, indicating that it takes time to experience positive health changes from pet ownership."

And they understand us, too. Not only what we're saying, but how we're saying it. "Dogs process both what we say and how we say it in a way which is amazingly similar to how human brains do," wrote Dr. Attila Andics, a neuroscientist at Eötvös Loránd University in Hungary. When dogs hear speech, he explained, they seem to separate the meaning of words from the intonation, and each aspect of speech is analyzed independently. The left hemisphere of the brain processes meaning, while intonation is analyzed in the right hemisphere.

Prior to this study, scientists believed only we humans had the ability to process meaning with the left hemispheres of our brains. That was even considered a major evolutionary leap for us humans. It turns out we shared this incredible leap with dogs.

I talk to my dogs and cats all the time. I have since I was a little girl gabbing away to Sparky.

Now, I keep up a constant prattle.

"Are you getting hungry, Coops? Of course you are. You're a dog. You're always hungry!"

Reading the news on my phone: "Can you believe this guy? No dog would've elected him. He's un-dog. What do you think?" I'm still waiting for his take on politics.

"Who's a good boy? Obviously it's you!"

"Oh, Coop," I sigh often. "What am I going to do?"

And the thing is, when I ask him that question, he usually gazes into my eyes with such adoration I end up walking away feeling like I can do anything. Regardless of the problem, he helps me solve it just by being there for me. Like any good friend.

Also, like any good friend, I make assumptions about what the animals around me would say in any given situation and often reply in "their" voice. (Think Sven in *Frozen*.)

"Coops, what would you like to do today?"

"Well, mama," I reply to myself using Cooper's voice, a particular mix of asthmatic and nasal, "I think I'd like to go for a run. Two miles or so. Then a snoozle in the sun. Then snacks and pets. Or whatever you want to do." I do it often enough, even my small daughters now reply to questions in their high-pitched version of the Cooper voice.

Every year, we took a long hike at a nearby nature preserve on Thanksgiving morning. We needed to exhaust Coop's energy before we left him at home for a few hours for dinner at my brother's, plus John and I wanted to burn off a few preemptive calories before we devoured all the pies.

We arrived at the typically quiet spot, and the parking lot was more than half full. Every other person and their dog had the same idea: burn off some steam before the festivities. On every trail we took, every turn and switchback, we encountered dog after dog after dog. Cooper doesn't handle dogs on trails well, so I spent the hike doubling back, stepping several feet off the trail, about-facing, and doling out as much squeeze cheese as I could to help him keep his head.

The can of squeeze cheese worked for a while. So did U-turns and circling back and zigzags and outright stopping while we waited for dogs to pass us. But, of course, he reached his maximum threshold at some point way in the back of the preserve, so I dragged him back to the car while fighting against his pulling, lunging, and barking. I ended up running him the whole way back to the parking lot. He focuses way better when he's running, though my shoulder and legs ached by the time I loaded him into the car.

The next day, we decided to pick out our Christmas tree. The Girl Scouts sell trees each year for a fundraiser, so we planned to hit the coffee shop across the street for hot chocolates, then pick out a tree and head home. As we loaded Violet, who was almost two at the time, into the car at the library with our plan in place, she looked up into my eyes and said, "Pooped." I rummaged around in the diaper bag. No diapers. Of course.

"We'll do the tree later," I said. John drove us straight home to change our toddler and put her down to nap.

It turned into a give-a-mouse-a-cookie situation: We might as well clean the house before we decorated, and since Violet tended to toss plates, bowls, spoons, and cups at that point in her toddlerhood, we needed to scrub down the walls and cabinets in the kitchen. I wanted everything clean before we put up the holiday decor, so it was a rush to scrub everything before naptime ended.

I sat on the floor, scouring the baseboards underneath the highchair with an eraser pad, when I felt a twinge. Just a small little tweak across my lower back. Not a big deal. Just a little ache.

My sister offered to watch Violet when she woke up from her nap so John and I could finish some errands. She stayed for dinner. We missed getting the tree but were ready to throw ourselves into full-blown Christmas Saturday morning.

I went to bed exhausted. Cooper curled up against the back of my legs, and I fell instantly to sleep—a rarity for me.

Around 1:30 a.m., I awoke with shooting, stabbing, spasming back pain. My left leg tingled. With every shift, pain sparked across my back and down my leg. In my pain- and sleep-induced fog, I decided if I could stretch out on the living room floor, I'd be okay. Trying to stand up, my back spasmed and I fell out of bed. I pushed up to my knees, braced myself on the edge of the bed, and shoved myself into a hunched-over-but-upright position. I shuffled my way across the floor. I scooched one foot, one inch at a time, then the other—until I made my way to the step leading into the living room. Reaching my foot down, my back spasmed, and I collapsed to the floor. Cooper popped out of bed and followed. He watched me struggle to flip myself over. He climbed up his chair in the living room and stared at me. Unblinking.

Once I succeeded in flattening myself to the floor, pushing through increasing pain with each inch, it grew worse by significant degrees. By then, it was so bad I couldn't get up even if I wanted to. I tried shifting, rolling, and scooching to the cabinet to grab the shelf to pull myself up. Every move I attempted made the pain worse. By then, my left leg felt entirely numb.

My plan had failed.

So, I turned to my beloved pup, who stayed by my side every minute of every day no matter what, and said, "Cooper, go get John."

He looked at me.

"Coop. Please. Get Papa."

He stared.

"OK, bubba. I'm dying here. I need help. Go. Get. John."

He jumped down from his chair, walked over, sniffed my face, and curled up alongside me and rested his head on my belly.

I couldn't move.

He got comfortable…

And fell asleep.

John found me two hours later in tears, cursing in the loudest whisper I could muster while Cooper snored softly by my side. Cooper's version of kindness was to cuddle me and keep me company until help arrived. He might not be Lassie, but he's all mine.

Despite his poor performance in my time of need, like any good friend, Cooper's presence feels reassuring. But unlike a human friend who I don't want around every second of every day, I love having Coop with me all the time. I don't even feel the same way about my human family members. I love them, but I don't want them with me all the time. Cooper? I don't mind his constant presence.

I know I'm not alone in this.

Researchers in the Netherlands wanted to find out if pet owners' emotional wellbeing was affected by having their pets around. In their paper, they wrote that conflicting evidence suggested pets helped with alleviating loneliness, improving self-esteem, lowering levels of depression, and creating higher levels of life satisfaction. However, evidence in other studies suggested pet owners were more likely to suffer from anxiety and depression. The researchers wanted to know which was more accurate: Do pets help our wellbeing or not?

Study participants volunteered to answer questions sent to their phones at ten random times throughout the day for the duration of the study. The survey asked if the pet was present and, if so, in an active role (like playing tug) or in a passive role (like sleeping on the couch next to you). Then it assessed how the person was feeling with a series of standardized questions.

What did they discover? If you share your home with a dog or cat, you won't be surprised to learn they concluded, "...the presence of a companion animal may buffer against negative feelings, while interacting with a companion animal may generate positive feelings."

What makes our pets such good friends? Why do most of us prefer the company of our dogs to the company of friends or family? Why are we happy to spend all our time with our dogs but not our human friends and family, who we also love but need time away from?

In part, I believe it's their unqualified acceptance of us as ourselves.

An unqualified acceptance that I don't share for myself. For instance, a thick, black hair pokes out from the corner of my chin. It grows from the same spot every few weeks, and the second I feel it poke up, I snag my tweezers and pull. That one tiny hair bugs me endlessly. I feel the edge of my chin to see if it's there at least once every day. If I think it might possibly be growing soon, I feel for it a dozen times a day. That one strand uses a small percentage of my brain power, taking up space and preoccupying me.

When I was in elementary school, the principal—a formidable nun who ran the school day with a giant bell in her hand—had thick hairs poking out of a mole on her chin. It caused endless speculation among the students. The hair added to our fear of her. In my mind, if left unchecked, my chin hair could approach the fearsomeness of Sister Marie Collette.

And yet. Even if I forgot to pluck it, Cooper would never notice. He loves me exactly as I am, chin hair and all. I know my human friends and family would notice it if I missed plucking it. Someone—my mom, my sister, John—would probably say, "Hey, you need to pluck that." Whereas, if Cooper noticed it and could talk, he would probably say, "I think your chin hair looks nice on you. Who cares anyway because you're perfect and I love you. Wanna go play tug?"

Dogs don't judge us. They don't assess our appearance. They don't consider the brand of shoes we wear to walk them or the color lipstick we put on for work. They don't care if we like bluegrass or hip hop, and they certainly don't care if we gain or lose a few pounds, wake up with frizzy hair, or get two giant pimples. None of it matters to them, which makes them incredibly valuable as friends.

Dogs love us for the people we actually are, for how we treat them, and for how we spend our time together. They'd be thrilled to walk alongside us in knee socks and sandals as long as we're walking together. They're equally happy to lounge on the couch with us in our favorite pilly, stretched-out sweatshirt from college, too. The outside stuff doesn't matter to our dogs, which is a needed reprieve and a release from the real world.

A dog stands by you. A dog encourages you to walk (or run) to be strong and healthy. A dog licks away your tears. A dog thinks you're perfect every single day, no matter what you look like or what you do, no matter if you feel brave and strong or if you hide in the girls' bathroom.

In my experience, a dog sees you even if everyone else overlooks you.

A dog knows you're beautiful because, even though a dog can't tell if you're wearing the "right" clothes or makeup, if you have your brows done, or if you have a thick hair poking out of your chin, a dog knows who you are. And that's where your beauty lies.

A dog simply says, over and over again, "I love you because you're you."

We all could use a friend like that.

CHAPTER 5

The Beautiful Mess of Being a Dog

Some moments divide our lives.

A few instances can split us into a before and an after. Most of those moments arrive unannounced. The phone rings. A letter arrives. There's a knock.

One moment you're living your before; the next, you're starting your after.

Mine arrived with a phone call the day after a mole biopsy on my back. "The doctor wants to discuss your results in person," the nurse said. "Can you come in today?"

I sat on the balcony off my bedroom. I stared out across the field in front of our house and tried to stay calm. But, of course, I knew. You don't see the doctor to receive test results unless they're bad. You don't get scheduled for a same-day appointment unless there's something really wrong.

It was the first week of December, but I don't remember it being cold. It probably was. At some point I texted John at work, gave the boys their see-you-later treats, climbed into my car, and drove to the doctor's office.

John met me there.

I liked my doctor. She balanced clinical professionalism with kindness. I trusted her. I never expected her to be the person who stood on the line that divided my before from my after. "I'm sorry," she said. She placed her hand on my knee.

She recommended a plastic surgeon. She recommended an oncologist. She reviewed the process and the steps and the outlook for the cancer she had just diagnosed me with. Although I heard her words, none of them sunk in.

We sat on the news for a couple days. Neither of us left the house. We cuddled the dogs on the couch and watched *Friends* reruns. We canceled our Christmas trip to visit John's family in Maryland.

We huddled on the couch for a few more days. We never talked about cancer. The dogs served as the only touchstone to real life during those days. They needed to go out in the morning, and they needed their bowls filled with breakfast. They needed to walk and to play. They needed their bowls filled again at dinnertime. They needed us. The dogs grounded us in normalcy. They kept us to a routine and reminded us that life moves forward.

On the day of my first surgery, we emerged from our initial fog. The first step, removing the tumor, wouldn't be a big deal—but I also needed to have a test to check my lymph nodes and see if the cancer had spread. Every doctor, specialist, nurse, surgeon, and oncologist repeated versions of the same refrain: "If there's nothing there, we'll get the tumor, and you'll be done."

Clean margins. Clean lymph node biopsy. Life goes on. I wanted to have one big surgery and move on with my life.

When they found cancer in my lymph nodes, it meant another surgery to remove the pocket of nodes in my left armpit, weeks of recovery with a horrible drain poking out my side, followed by another surgery to install a port in my chest so I could begin a year of chemo.

During all those appointments and surgeries and medications and next steps and consultations, we were so busy, we never had time to think. We drove from doctor's office to doctor's office. We booked the dogs at doggy daycare when we needed to stay overnight at the hospital. Our incredible friend and professional pet sitter, Ann, jumped in to walk the boys and bring me ginger ale, as did our generous friends and neighbors. My book club came and did our yard work. Meanwhile, John and I existed in a haze of appointments and fear.

Each time I came home from an appointment or a procedure, all I wanted was to snuggle with the dogs in a big pile on my bed. I wanted their warmth and solid heft to anchor me. I started to joke with friends: All I had to do to get John to lift his "no dogs on the bed" rule was get cancer.

The nurse called to reschedule my port surgery. "I just noticed it's on your birthday," she said. "You can't have surgery on your birthday! How about the day after?" I wasn't sure it mattered. I went the day after and the surgeon installed my port.

I started chemo at the end of February. For the first month, my protocol included sitting in an armchair in the oncologist's office while an IV dripped into the port in my chest. I could read, watch TV, chat with John or the nurses, bring work—anything sedentary to pass those hours each day. More jokes: All I had to do to get a couple quiet hours to myself to drink coffee and read was get cancer.

At the same time, John's PhD program at the university drew to a close. He needed to find a job, and he needed to find one quickly. It was February, and he only had until May to stay in his department. As a freelancer, I survived—*literally* now—on his university-provided health insurance benefits. During that month of two-hour daily infusions, John searched for a job. He sent countless queries and ultimately was offered a postdoc spot at a lab in southern Louisiana.

We debated what to do. I got sicker. I lost my hair. I lost my appetite. I lost weight. I felt like I had the flu constantly. Yet, a horrifying deadline loomed. I needed chemo, and I needed health insurance to get it. John's new job would provide insurance, but it was in a small town so far away from the friends helping us through this. Could I possibly get my treatment there, or would I have to somehow drive myself the hour to New Orleans or another city for care? Did I want to be somewhere unknown and feel this bad? Could we find anyone to help with the dogs down there?

Ultimately, we realized I couldn't get my treatment there. I couldn't be somewhere unknown and sick without family and friends to jump in and help. I couldn't trust a stranger to walk the dogs when side effects left me too sick to take them out. But I needed chemo, and I needed health insurance to get the chemo, so John accepted the job in Houma, Louisiana, while I remained in Indiana with the boys.

He leased an apartment sight unseen over the phone. He filled out his HR paperwork while I sat in the cancer center getting my daily two-hour chemo infusion. He loaded his Saturn Ion with an inflatable mattress, a stool, clothes, a set of dishes and cutlery, a lamp, and reference books. He planned to buy a futon when he arrived in Louisiana two days later. We held each other while we cried. Then, he left. I was so sick, I went straight back to bed.

I still had eleven months of treatment ahead of me.

After the first month of daily infusions, I learned how to give myself a shot. I needed to inject my stomach or thigh with the take-home version of my chemo three times a week. "Give it right before bed," a kind nurse suggested. "The side effects will lessen overnight."

Monday, Wednesday, and Friday nights, between 8:00 and 9:00, I pulled a syringe out of the butter dish in my fridge, injected myself with chemo, and went to sleep.

Cooper and Lucas cuddled in bed with me each night. Cooper slept curled up next to my head right on John's pillow, and Lucas slept across the foot of the bed, his enormous head resting on my ankles. Emmett, who hated being hot, slept in a ball on the foot of the chaise in the corner of our bedroom—within reach, but not touching the rest of us. Until my side effects worsened.

Many chemo nights, I experienced a bone-chilling cold. No matter how many layers of sweaters I put on or how many blankets I tossed over the bed, I couldn't warm up. Even when I switched on my heating pad, I still shivered. My teeth chattered. I'd wrap a scarf around my neck and try to bury myself deep under the blanket pile. On those nights, Lucas shifted from the foot of the bed and positioned himself along my left side. Cooper moved to my right side. Emmett jumped off the chaise and climbed onto the bed. He splayed across the foot of the bed, warming my feet. Unbidden, the dogs piled on me. I rattled from the chills, but their steadfast warmth and the heft of their bodies eventually lulled me back to sleep.

Some nights brought the opposite: night sweats. On those nights, I'd wake up to find Coop on the pillow, near me but not touching. Emmett snored on the chaise, and Lucas stretched out at the foot of the opposite side of the bed. I wondered if

I radiated so much heat they naturally shifted away, or if they sensed something they couldn't understand. How did they know which nights required their persistent snuggles and which nights didn't? Could they sense my body temperature and adjust their behavior accordingly? Or were they smelling something changing in my body chemistry on chemo nights?

It wasn't an impossible or even improbable thought. Dogs sense things—like the earliest stages of cancer—in ways we can't begin to imagine or understand. In fact, researchers have experimented with dogs' highly advanced sense of smell to detect various cancers with great success. In trials, dogs sniffed out breast and lung cancer on a person's breath. Others detected bladder and prostate cancers by smelling the patients' urine. Still other dogs found colorectal cancer, ovarian cancer, and more by sniffing blood samples or biopsies.

Dogs' sense of smell is estimated to be 100 million times more sensitive than our own. Chances are, if I would've known how to ask them, and if they would've known how to answer, my dogs might've been able to alert me to my cancer before my doctor.

Could they also sense my body temperature fluctuations? Researchers recently discovered that dogs do detect heat, but not by using their skin receptors. Instead, it's their powerful noses again. Two studies showed that, like bats, dogs can sense heat. This likely developed among their wolf ancestors to help them find warm-bodied prey. Now, their unique heat-sensing ability helped me stay warm when bone-rattling chills shook my body.

It's possible, too, that they understood the stress and pain of my experience. There's a psychological concept called "theory of mind," which means you can understand mental states—your own and others'. It develops in human children around four or five. At that age, kids start to understand how other people think and feel. They start to understand beliefs—theirs and others'—and that seeing is knowing. It's an important set of cognitive functions for playing pretend, telling or understanding stories, holding conversations, and even making friends.

Our dogs don't play pretend or tell stories, but can they understand our mental states? On the days I couldn't drag myself out of bed, the nights I couldn't sleep because of temperature fluctuations, or the morning I sobbed because my hair started to fall out in the shower, did they have a sense of my state of mind? Or were they simply reacting to my hormones, my temperature, my scent?

No study has shown dogs have theory of mind, though none have shown they don't, either. In fact, some studies have attempted to test dogs' understanding of what others do and do not understand; however, researchers like dog pro Alexandra Horowitz argue these tests—called "perspective-taking" tests—aren't relevant to dog subjects like they are to human subjects. In a response to one such study, Horowitz wrote, "None of the canid research to date has made a claim to have proven (or disproven) that dogs have a theory of mind. However, using the experimental paradigms developed thus far, there is no chance that any research *could* legitimately make such a claim."

But dogs *do* pay attention to what we pay attention to, and they react accordingly. They do know when someone is trying to be deceptive by hiding a treat under one cup but indicating another. They *appear* to know how we're feeling; I saw the proof over and over again as Emmett worked as a therapy dog with children who were suffering. He seemed to know how to react based on what different children needed. And I saw it every single day as Emmett, Lucas, and Cooper shepherded me through nausea, exhaustion, stress, and anxiety. They perceived something about me that caused them to react appropriately, theory of mind or not.

To get through each day, I established a routine: I woke up early, usually with the sun. We four trudged downstairs, and I opened the back door to let the boys out. As I made their breakfast, I started my coffee. I let the dogs back in, they ate, and we went back upstairs. Mornings ran in this cycle for months. I took a nap around 10:00 every morning, and they napped with me. Our morning nap became so routine that, as soon as I closed my laptop, they dashed from the office to the bedroom, jumping into their spots on my bed before I was even out of my chair.

Whole days passed without me speaking to or seeing another human. When I drove up to Indianapolis for appointments at the cancer center, I'd book the dogs in doggy daycare or hire Ann to walk them. Hours later, I returned home either with the boys from daycare pickup or they'd greet me at the door. I'd fill their bowls and collapse on the couch. As soon as they finished eating, they'd jump up, each into his preferred spot, and the four of us would stay snuggled, safe and secure in our little world, until bedtime.

I created a series of weekly and daily habits to stave off the real fear of dying. I took Lucas and Cooper to daycare once a week because they needed to burn off steam, but Emmett had no interest in playing with other dogs. He preferred to stay home with me. I chipped away at freelance work, though I eventually gave up sitting at my desk in my office and instead brought my laptop into bed to work under a fluffy pile of blankets and dogs.

When it was nice, I wrote outside on the patio while the boys ran, dug up flowers, or lounged in sunspots.

John visited when he could, usually for one weekend every six or eight weeks. The dogs lost their minds when he walked in the door. They leapt all over him and each other. Lucas howled. Cooper barked. Emmett wagged his tail so hard he often slipped and fell. John would take care of stuff around the house for a couple days, then he'd fly back to Louisiana, and the dogs and I would return to our quiet routine.

All the while, Cooper's behavior deteriorated. His anxiety skyrocketed. He watched me closely and followed me everywhere. When I showered, he curled up on the bathmat. When I walked to the kitchen to get a coffee, he trailed me. When I collected the mail from the box out front, he watched from the front window.

The summer before my diagnosis, a month before Cooper turned one, I enrolled him in a trick training class. He'd already aced puppy kindergarten and basic obedience. He learned tricks and behaviors in a fraction of the time it took the big boys to learn them. He exhausted my basic skills as a handler. So, to trick class we went. He learned them all. Every single trick. He mastered them faster than I did; Cooper's brilliance overcame the clumsiness of his handler.

Then Cooper had his first birthday and my diagnosis followed. Around the time chemo started, he hit a developmental milestone. Dogs go through a couple distinct "fear periods"— one as a small pup between eight and ten weeks, and one in adolescence, usually between six and fourteen months. During the fear period, dogs become highly sensitive, suspicious, and reactive. It's a normal part of development, and—as long as everything stays calm and stable during the few weeks of fear—everything goes back to normal. Your dog might not have been afraid of an umbrella before his fear period. He gets spooked by one during his fear period. Everyone stays cool; the fear passes.

"The dangerous part is this: during this particular developmental stage, your dog's brain is on a hair trigger, exquisitely sensitive to anything 'bad' that may happen. A single frightening or painful experience during the fear period can have a lasting impact for the rest of your dog's life," wrote veterinarian and professional dog trainer Jennifer L. Summerfield.

Cooper's second fear period coincided with my battle with cancer. Prior to this, Cooper walked through life behind Emmett and Lucas. We socialized him to all sorts of things, and the only thing we noticed through all our training and socialization exercises that struck us as odd was the severity of his startle reflex. He startled easily and took longer to recover, even longer than Lucas, our "reactive dog."

For his first year with us, John walked Cooper to Petco to get his nails cut twice a month. The round trip clocked in at about two miles. They'd wander the aisles while he waited his turn. He'd get his nails cut. John would buy him a treat or a toy, then they'd walk home.

Months later, we couldn't take Coop into Petco at all—especially for a nail trim—because he'd bark and yip and lunge at the other customers. We couldn't walk him down a crowded sidewalk because he'd launch onto his hind legs and bark at passing dogs. When he returned home, he played with his brothers. He played with me. He cuddled. He worked. We continued to train tricks and worked on obedience stuff at home. But he was no longer the happy, playful, outgoing puppy he once was.

At the time, I had no idea what was wrong. It was only in retrospect that I understood how my diagnosis impacted him during this developmentally appropriate fear period. Combined with his wonky DNA that we were only beginning to unravel, hitting a fear period when things were scary made him, well…scared.

The mystery of his genetic background unraveled more with an unexpected email from his rescue. Two of Cooper's littermates were euthanized for extreme behavior, including killing other animals and biting people severely enough to require stitches. At the time of the email, the rescue had received similar reports of behavior problems from two other littermates, though their fate was unknown. The volunteer from the rescue felt it was her responsibility to let the other littermates' adopters know, though she wasn't able to track down everyone. She said it was in the best interest of safety to fully disclose what she knew.

I replied to the email, thanking her for her hard work. I filled her in on Cooper: *He's fearful,* I wrote, *and shy of strangers. At doggy daycare, he thrives, and he loves cuddling people at home. I'll continue to train with him, doubling down on my efforts,* I promised.

Cooper touched his nose to my cheek. I didn't budge, so he pushed his cold, wet snout against my face. I groaned. Rolled over. Lifted the comforter and quilt. He squirmed under and pressed his back into mine. I tucked the blankets around him, pulled the remaining bits around my shoulder, and slid back into sleep.

Throughout the night, Cooper kicked me as he ran and twitched—as most dogs do—in slumber. His nails dug into my back. He stood up, twirled three times, and settled in with an elbow jammed into my ribcage. Later, he stretched his full length, jabbing me with his nails before contracting into a tiny ball with his head poking out of the quilt. I awoke in the dark with his hot breath puffing into my face as we now shared my pillow.

He does this every night.

He falls asleep on the chair in the corner of our bedroom. We tuck a huge comforter around him. He snores softly. Then, several hours later, after I've fallen fitfully asleep, I feel his icy nose press into my cheek, and the routine begins. By the time the alarm goes off, he's bright-eyed and ready to face the day, while I slug down cup after cup of coffee just to have enough energy to brush my teeth.

And yet, I would never kick him out. Non-dog people often ask me: Why don't you make him sleep in the living room? Why do you allow this to happen each night?

Well, I say, I want him to be happy.

Most of us sacrifice our own comfort to some degree for someone else's happiness, and you don't even consider it—not really—until someone else questions it.

I stick to my convictions. I know I'd sleep better if I didn't allow these nightly acrobatics, but it's lovely having him squished against me. And it makes him happy.

I love the mystery of the human-animal bond. It fascinates me to see the extraordinary lengths people go to ensure an animal's happiness, or at least our assumption of their happiness. We don't know what they're thinking, of course. I don't know if Cooper appreciates me lifting up the covers for him each night or if he's driven purely by a sense of having his own needs met. He's cold and he thinks, "This is what I need and this is how I get it." Whether he has a developed theory of mind or not, whether he can understand my exhaustion or discomfort, it doesn't matter. If he pushes his nose into my cheek so that I lift up the comforter and let him crawl under solely because he's cold and wants to be warm, so be it. It warms me up, too. Chemo turned me into a bad sleeper anyway.

"There's a cat in my living room."

I heard the tension in John's voice on the phone, but I couldn't wrap my mind around what he was saying.

"What?"

"A cat! There's a small black cat standing in my living room."

I paused. "Okay," I said. "How?"

He stammered the story: Moments before, he heard meowing outside his door. He opened up to peek, and there stood a tiny black kitten. She took one look at him and waltzed in.

He assumed she was a few months old. Her petite, slender body and enormous, triangular ears belied her age. He would later learn she was about a year old, but her tiny stature—and the mischievous personality he'd soon discover—made her seem kitten-like.

Summers in Louisiana sizzle. The scorched ground and oppressive humidity turn people into water bugs, skittering from one air-conditioned location to the next. This kitten, John knew, needed help to survive the mid-July heat. So, after he hung up the phone, he drove to the nearest pet store and stocked up on cat stuff: a litter box and litter, cans of food, toys, and a water dish.

In Houma, the southern Louisiana town where John lived, and in Cocodrie, the even-farther-south town where he worked, strays lurked around every corner. He knew by sight the ferals who lived in and around his apartment complex. This cat, though, he'd never seen before. He assumed she was a pet and someone was looking for her. He hung up signs, posted online, and joined a lost pets Facebook group. She was sweet, he said, and looked fairly healthy, so she had to have people, right?

Yet, as much as he wanted to help her, he also didn't want her. When John was a child, he developed a fear of his aunt's cats, who swiped and bit at his legs. That ultimately developed into a general fear of cats he masked by telling everyone he was allergic.

I'd always wanted a cat, but I could never get John on board. Because of his fear of cats, it shocked and delighted me when he welcomed this small cat into his place even temporarily. He called her Newt, a nod to *Aliens*, his favorite sci-fi movie.

John spent the next few months terrified of his new roommate. He slept with his bedroom door closed, was afraid to pet her, and had no idea how to spend time with her. Meanwhile, he searched for her family.

Weeks passed. No one called.

"Toss her in the bayou," folks told him. "Alligator food," they said.

Meanwhile, he called around and booked her a checkup with a veterinarian. Newt had worms and fleas. She was underweight. She wasn't spayed, and on the day of her procedure, she cried in her crate so mournfully and broke John's heart so completely that he called me later the same afternoon and said, "Okay. So, we have a cat."

When he picked her up after her spay, she hadn't fully recovered from the anesthesia. She crawled into his arms, and he cradled her like a baby until she awoke fully.

When his next trip back to Indiana was imminent, John realized he needed someone to watch Newt. He interviewed pet sitters, and during their first meeting, one pet sitter played with Newt and scratched her belly.

"Aren't you afraid she'll bite you?" John asked.

"No," the pet sitter laughed. "Newtkins is the sweetest!" He tickled her belly again and tossed a piece of crumpled paper that Newt chased and pounced and kicked. John hired him on the spot.

Newt quickly became John's "princess." He spoiled her with treats and toys, and talked about her nonstop. When he flew back to Indiana, as soon as his plane landed, he'd whip out his phone and show me dozens of pictures of Newt doing cat things. "Here she is asleep on the futon, and here she is playing with her pouncer, and here she is just sitting there."

When he was back in Louisiana, he'd regale me with Newt stories each night on Skype. He'd pan the camera around the living room so I could watch her pounce on her toys or, more often, sit perfectly still and stare at John. Sometimes he'd set up his laptop so that I could watch him play with her and her teaser toy. "Look how high she can jump!"

He texted me daily with pictures of her playing with feathers and jumping in and out of a packing box. He emailed me from work with funny stories from Newt's day: "She figured out how to open the kitchen cabinets, so now she pops out to startle me. I think she does it to be funny."

Newt started a daily game of "hide the dish sponge." When John left for work in the morning, the sponge sat on the drying rack in the sink. Late afternoon, he'd return home and the sponge would be gone. He'd poke around to find it, then return it to the sink, only for Newt to repeat the game the next day. It made John happy; he'd text me the locations of the pilfered sponge most weekdays.

She also chewed through the cord to the ceiling fan, which lost him his security deposit. She popped his air mattress, so he spent the rest of his time in the apartment sleeping on the floor. Newt, meanwhile, slept on the cushy futon. I teased John about being too afraid to cuddle with her to sleep on the futon mattress. He was afraid she might bite him, he said, like if he rolled over on her in the night. But, he said, he was finally comfortable enough to swap his jeans for a pair of shorts; by now, he was pretty sure she wasn't going to attack his legs.

He developed nicknames for her: Newtie, Newtie-tootie, Newtie-tootie-fresh-and-fruity, Newtles (sounds like "noodles"), Toots, Toots McGoots, and Newtkins, the name bestowed by the pet sitter. Most often, though, he called her, "my pretty, pretty princess."

And every day upon his return home from the lab, he'd open the door to Newt, sitting on the other side of the door awaiting his return.

One crisp fall morning, I sat in my oncologist's waiting room with my mom. The week prior, I underwent another CT scan to see if the cancer had spread to my lungs or abdomen. While I waited to be called back into the exam room, my phone dinged. It dinged again. And again. I pulled it out of my purse and opened my messaging app.

John had texted a string of photos—Newt with her tongue stuck out from three different angles. I laughed. I turned the phone to my mom to show her the silly photos. My mom smiled.

"That cat," she said, "is John's guardian angel."

The whole year passed me by; almost as suddenly as it began, I pulled my very last shot out of the butter dish I used to store my chemo needles. I gave myself the final injection and burst into tears.

"I'm done!" I shouted. I leaped into the air and jumped around. "I'm done!" The dogs startled awake from their spots on the couch, but quickly settled back in as I danced around the kitchen singing, "I'm done! I'm done! I'm done!" I pushed the needle into my sharps disposal containers and called John. I needed to cheer or celebrate with someone, but he didn't answer. So, I gathered the dogs around me and cried tears of relief into their necks. They gave me the friendship I needed that night.

Chemo was done, but I knew my fate for the next five years: quarterly CT scans, blood draws, X-rays, exams. But no more chemo. I could take any test, any scan, *anything*, but I was done with my chemo shots.

I packed up the house and the dogs, and we drove down to Houma, Louisiana, where we'd all live for the next two years. While I was looking forward to this next chapter for our family, I didn't yet know cancer wasn't done with us. It wasn't going to leave our family alone. It was lurking behind the scenes, waiting to attack again.

I finally met Newt the following summer. I finished chemo at the end of February—exactly one year from my first injection—and it took three months to pack up our Indy house, find a rental in Louisiana that accepted three big dogs and a cat, and hire movers to cross those 900 miles.

John moved in a few weeks ahead of time to help Newt adjust to her new home and to set up the basics. Then he flew up to drive from Indy to Houma with me and the dogs.

We drove the eighteen hours over two days, and when we arrived at the rental, John took the dogs in the yard while I went inside to meet Newtie, one-on-one. I perched on the edge of the futon. She eyed me while I held still, letting her set the pace.

She crept over and sniffed my hand. I didn't move or speak until I felt like she grew bored of me. As she started to walk away, having thoroughly gotten a whiff of me, I whispered to her, "Thank you, Newt. Thank you for keeping John safe."

And I silently apologized for the next chapter ahead of her and the three dogs she was about to meet.

Dogs make interspecies friends all the time. The internet leads us to believe there's a dog for every orphaned goat, elephant, and piglet. My dogs, however, never experienced interspecies relationships. Unless you count the time Emmett and Lucas tried to chase stray cats in our old DC neighborhood.

Luckily, we rented an enormous old house with lots of space to arrange the animals safely. It was the only house available in town that allowed us to have three dogs and one cat; in fact, the landlord said he didn't care at all, which should have been a red flag. The house was falling apart. The roof leaked in several spots. ("Yeah, it does that," the landlord said when I called him to report the leaks.) The floors sunk in some spots and lifted in others. The windows and doors sat loose in their frames, so the house creaked and leaked and blew with every gust of wind or rainfall. The day after we moved in, we found underwear in the garden, a rotten lizard in the kitchen cupboard, and a freezer stocked full of ducks. I texted the landlord. He picked up the ducks.

Despite its many flaws, the house accommodated the animals. The first floor was divided into two sections. In the front, a squat porch dangled off the foundation and led into a "formal" dining room and a sitting room. We kept those rooms closed off and never could use the front door; it had no handle on the outside. Swinging doors separated the front half from the kitchen, breakfast room, master bedroom, and bathroom. A hallway led in one direction toward the garage, laundry room, and backyard, and in the other direction up a set of stairs. Those stairs led to an enormous room we dubbed "the big room." This room quickly became the hub of activity for us. I moved my desk into one corner. We set up a living room on one side, and a table and bookcase lined the back wall of windows. From the corner where my desk sat, another flight of stairs led up to the third floor, which included three bedrooms, a bathroom, and a terrifying ladder into an attic we were afraid to enter. With all the twists and turns, separate rooms, and doors between every space in the house, we figured out how to give everyone controlled freedom.

First, we turned one of the third floor bedrooms into Newt's lair. We stocked it with her toys, cat tree, food and water dishes, and tucked a litter box into a closet. A baby gate in the entrance ensured none of the dogs could gain access to her space. I gated off the stairs from the big room to the third floor. The dogs had access to the big room and everything below, while Newt had access to the whole house with gates to retreat behind if the dogs acted up.

This space would serve us well over and over again. When John picked up stray dog Molly, we were able to keep her in the front two rooms so she had plenty of space to herself while Newt was out. Then, even later, when stray kitten Petey joined the fray, she held dominion over the third floor bathroom.

It was bonkers, but it worked.

Meanwhile, I slowly integrated the dogs with Newt. Emmett met her, gave the Emmett equivalent of a shoulder shrug, and that was that. Newt quickly realized he was safe to be around because he pretended she didn't exist. He steadfastly ignored her presence, even when she swatted, chewed, and pounced on his tail. She sat next to him on his bed. She head-booped him once, the only time she ever head-booped—the equivalent of a kitty hug—a dog. Yet he ignored her. Maybe that's why she liked him so much; she was guaranteed her space and her preferences. Even when she played with his tail, rolling around and biting it, kicking it with her back feet and chewing the fuzzy tip, he sat still and pretended she wasn't there.

Cooper took longer. We kept him on leash and allowed Newt to approach or retreat however she wanted while I gave Coop piles of treats.

He wasn't sure: friend or foe? One minute he'd sniff her, the next he'd lunge. She wasn't sure about him either. She tried to bat his tail like she did Emmett's, but she'd get scared and leap up to bite his thigh. Their relationship shifted suddenly when they both realized they loved to skitter. Then, Newt and Coop played. They chased each other around the circular table in the middle of the big room. She'd gain the higher ground of a chair and swat his nose. He'd nuzzle her belly. She'd jump down and dash away with him in pursuit. Every day they played this game, all the while I held my breath because he was so much bigger than Newt. But, of course, she ran the show, and when the game was done for her, she'd bite him or swat him hard enough to send him away.

Lucas, though, made things difficult. Of course he did.

The second he spotted Newt, he wanted to eat her. We didn't let him get near enough to even touch a fur on her little body, though he certainly tried. For months he stayed on leash anytime the door to the third floor was open. I felt like we weren't making any progress despite daily training, so I started calling cat experts and read every cat behavior book I could get my hands on.

At mealtimes, we fed the dogs in a line across a blue floral runner that spanned the length of our kitchen. Most cat owners we knew told us cats wouldn't eat breakfast and dinner with the dogs; they preferred to eat bites whenever they were hungry. Newt, though, broke the mold. She wanted to eat her breakfast and dinner with the dogs. She wanted to eat it in a bowl with them, and if we didn't put it down fast enough, she'd shove a dog—usually Emmett—out of the way to start in on his food.

So I started feeding them all at the same time. I scooped the dogs' food and supplements into their bowls, but before I set the bowls on the rug—lest Newt push her face in and start devouring their kibble—I scooped her wet food into a dish and placed it on top of the refrigerator. She'd leap up onto the counter, then onto the fridge, and start gobbling up her pâté. Meanwhile, Lucas finished his bowl in a few big gulps. Then he followed me to the sink where I'd hold the cat food spoon down to his level and let him lick it clean before putting it all in the dishwasher. By the time he finished, Emmett, Cooper, and Newt were nearly done with their dinners, none the wiser. It became a ritual, just for me and him. The cat food spoon probably softened Lucas toward Newt, too.

Meanwhile, Newt worked on training Lucas in her own way. She ignored him completely. Even when he lunged at her or tried to chase her up the stairs, she'd sit calmly on the other side of the dividing gate and gaze at him. She never hissed or swatted at him like she did with Emmett and Cooper. She simply assessed him from a safe distance. We'd rein him in and work on rewarding him for ignoring her, and she continued to watch calmly, coolly nearby. After almost six months, we noticed a shift in their interactions: He still lunged at her or chased her up the stairs and through her gate, but there wasn't any force or gusto behind it, and she didn't run too fast to get away. It was clear he continued to chase her because now he thought it was fun.

Most days, Newt sauntered into the big room and looked around. Lucas lazed on the couch with one eye open, trained on her. As soon as she started across the space, he pounced, sending her fleeing back upstairs. He wagged his tail and trotted back to the couch while she peered through her gate. Eventually she stopped retreating because he skidded to a stop before he ever reached her, and somehow—despite my months of research and training—they figured their relationship out on their own.

By the time John found Petey, the stray kitten stranded in the middle of the highway, Lucas and Newt were so solid together, I often discovered them sleeping side by side at the foot of our bed. When the tiny, four-week-old kitten arrived, I felt confident in Emmett's and Cooper's reactions, but I debated about Lucas. Would he apply the cat training we did over the first six months with Newt? Or would this be all new since it was a new cat—and a kitten at that?

Petey lived in the third floor bathroom. She needed to be separated from Newt until we knew her health status, but the vet okayed us introducing the dogs. We decided to do it one at a time, with the most reliable to the least, so we could gauge Petey's reaction to the dogs. If she seemed terrified, we'd slow the pace. If she seemed fine, we'd keep at it.

We brought Emmett in first, who rolled his eyes. He looked at me, looked at John, sighed, then left the room.

Cooper nosed her while she batted his snout. His extreme interest gave way to her playfulness. Petey immediately trusted Cooper to be a friend. She climbed on his back and nibbled at his ears. She swatted his tail. We put Newt in her bedroom and latched the door so we could let Petey and Cooper chase each other up and down the hallway. Like sticking two babies in a sandbox, they were instant playmates.

Lucas took a turn after he had a long walk to burn off some energy. We leashed him up, grabbed cans of spray cheese, and led him to the bathroom. He sniffed under the door and started to whine. I scooped up Petey and John held Lucas. Lucas took one look at the kitten and swiveled his head to John to get his cheese reward. The cat training we did with Newt paid off. He did exactly what we spent all those months working on; instead of staring down the cat, he automatically performed his "watch me" cue and turned to look at John and collect his treat.

Within a few days of repeated short bursts of exposure, Petey was able to come down the stairs to the second floor and spend chunks of time hanging out in the big room with one or two dogs at a time.

I knew Lucas would never be an interspecies bestie like the dogs on the internet. It took hard work to make him comfortable around the cats. But it did work.

As I watched Lucas allow Petey to bat his tail, it hit me how far my big yellow dog had come since those first terrifying months. Regardless of all the other successes we'd had, watching him coexist with a kitten helped me to see how much potential he truly had within him. I wondered how much more was under the surface. If he could befriend a cat and a kitten, what else could he do?

I would soon find out.

The first spring in Houma, I took Emmett and Lucas to the vet to have lumps removed. As dogs age, they grow lots of lumps; most are benign pockets of fat called lipomas, and some are cysts or warts common with aging bodies.

The vet sent the lumps off for labs, but the surgeries went well. The vet wasn't available when I arrived for pickup, so I took my sleepy, post-anesthesia boys and headed home. Later that night, she called to say she wanted to see Emmett for a follow-up in a couple days, so I scheduled his appointment with the front desk and thanked my lucky stars Lucas didn't need one, too. Taking him to the vet was such an ordeal every time, so the fewer trips, the better.

A few days later, while I sat in the lobby with Emmett, the veterinary student working with our vet came out and said he just got off the phone with the lab, and had great news: Lucas's results were clear. A plain old lump. No further action needed!

Then, the veterinarian walked out of her office.

"Emmett's results are in." She paused. "Why don't you come on back and we can talk about this."

We sat down in an exam room and she led me through what we faced: He was diagnosed with an insidious, aggressive form of cancer called hemangiosarcoma, which affects the lining of his blood cells. As soon as we discussed the pathology results, the vet took him straight back to X-ray his heart, liver, and spleen, and to look for fluid build ups. Because the cancer is so aggressive, often the first sign is far too late and the organs are riddled with tumors. Thankfully, there weren't any visible tumors, though, she cautioned, X-rays would only show large tumors. We also needed ultrasounds.

The front desk staff scheduled us with the veterinary oncologist the following week. Our plan was for the oncologist to do a physical exam, review his results, and help us determine the best course of action.

While we waited for his oncology appointment, I cried more over Em's diagnosis than I did the entire fifteen months I went through my own surgeries and treatment.

When Emmett was much younger, he had a cancerous growth on his leg. The oncologist we met with at that time said our best option was to remove his leg. The surgeon disagreed. He felt he could safely remove the tumor and preserve the leg. We spent sleepless nights preparing for the worst; if it turned out during surgery he did need to lose the leg, we wanted to be prepared. Of course, the surgeon was right. He completed the procedure and preserved the leg. For the next two years, we took Emmett to the oncologist for imaging and nothing ever came of it. Cancer free, the oncologist declared.

My anger surged with this new diagnosis.

It's not fair. He's already had cancer.

"At least" are the two most insidious words in English. Probably in other languages, too, but I don't know many other languages.

At least they caught it early.

At least it wasn't worse.

At least he didn't suffer.

At least says, "It could've been worse." At least says, "Quit complaining." At least says, "I see your suffering, but it's not as bad as it could've been. Move on." At least says, "Oh, yeah? Well, I've had it worse. Let me tell you about suffering."

It's unsympathetic. It's unempathetic. It's unkind.

In our family, we have a rule: No comparative suffering. Just because something bad happened to me at some point—just because I had cancer, for instance—doesn't mean I can belittle John when he's violently ill with the flu. "Oh, you have a fever? Chills? Vomiting? At least you're not going through chemo."

It's unhelpful. It's also really jerky.

When Emmett received his second cancer diagnosis, we got a lot of at leasts. "At least he lived a long life." A dog's life is never long enough. Ever. "At least he lived a good life." Sure, but I don't view that as a fair exchange for saying goodbye to my best friend. "At least you can always get another dog to honor his life." Are you kidding me? "At least you get a little more time together." While, sure, that's true, truth telling and compassion don't need to be mutually exclusive.

A kinder response would have been, "I'm so sorry. This is terrible. I'm so grateful for Emmett. I can only imagine what you're going through. I'll think of a way to help, but if there's something specific you need, please ask."

Once we realized the severity of Emmett's diagnosis—a few months, maybe, a year if we were lucky—I decided whatever time he had left would be spent doing only the things he loved. It started with a box of steaks my brother and sister-in-law mailed to him. We grilled one up for him that night.

Emmett's cancer meant a big adjustment to my schedule. He needed regular blood checks at his local vet and quarterly checks at the oncologist. I drove him back and forth, chatted with the techs and vets about my wonderful boy, and squeezed in my work while I waited for him to come out of ultrasounds. I found a rhythm to managing his appointments against all of my own blood tests and quarterly checks at the oncologist, the dermatologist, and the radiologist.

"We make quite the pair," I said to him in the car on the way to his blood test.

Later that month, I took Emmett to his blood check. His platelets tanked. The vet placed him on immediate restriction: no playing, no walking, no exercise at all. He needed to rest, and the risk of an internal bleed rocketed sky-high. If an internal bleed happened, he would die.

All our tests so far had been unremarkable. Until those results came in, we continued with life, almost forgetting he carried the weight of terminal cancer. These results floored me and John, pulling down the veil of denial we had so carefully put up. They stopped his chemo temporarily, until we could see if his platelets would recover. I started to panic about him not getting his chemo, about this reprieve from fighting the cancer to give his body a rest. I wanted him to rest, but I wanted him to win this battle.

Nodules on his spleen and liver appeared. We knew the risks of this cancer—sudden death from a bleed out—but everything had been so normal that we conveniently pushed those facts aside. When his platelets tanked, icy fear crept up my spine. I sat on his bed and rubbed his belly to keep him still; I needed to feel his solid frame, his muscles, his soft fur under my hand. To know he was there. To know he was whole.

At his recheck, his counts improved. We kept him resting, restarted his chemo, and his counts continued to restore to normal levels. He came off restriction. My dread retreated but never again fully disappeared.

Whole days would go by where the normalcy of our routine pulled me from the fear of him suddenly dying from a bleed. Whole days would go by where the steady rhythm of administering his meds and taking care of everyone prevented me from focusing too much on the terminal reality of his disease. Other days, it would sneak up on me. I'd cry into the thick fur around his neck. I'd lament about how unfair it all was. Then, I'd shake it off. Rinse my face. Give him a treat. Move forward.

Still, cancer still wasn't done with us.

CHAPTER 6

Steady Paws: Dogs You Can Count On

One sweltering Saturday shortly before his retirement as a therapy dog, Emmett and I volunteered at the county fair. We staffed a humane association booth filled with educational materials, pet adoption promotion, and a lucky duck game for kids. The game was a big hit, and we doled out prizes nonstop. Most of the people who chatted were polite and friendly and asked if they could pat Emmett. I loved outreach events like this because they were low-key conversations—much more comfortable for me than standing in front of an audience—and these events genuinely made a difference.

A tired-looking, middle-aged woman ambled over and told me she never had her outdoor cat spayed because she thought it was unlikely she'd get pregnant. But just last night the cat came to the door with a kitten in her mouth. Then she went and got a second kitten. She had birthed a litter of kittens, but those two were the only survivors. "I can't keep them," she said, "and I don't know how to get my cat spayed."

She asked me what would happen if she couldn't afford to spay her cat. If she didn't, could the cat give birth to another litter? I explained to her that, yes, unaltered cats can and do have many litters over a lifetime. I passed along a brochure about a low-cost spay clinic. I provided her with the phone number of the shelter to call about the kittens. As she slouched away, I hoped she'd follow through.

Another woman told me she knew a man on her street hosted dog fights in his basement. She called the police, as did several other neighbors, but the police didn't go into the house. She said the police showed up, questioned the guy at his front door, and left. Livid that they didn't even enter the property, she said she felt helpless, like there was nothing she could do. She was afraid for her children's safety—one of the guy's dogs had gotten out one day and ripped around the neighborhood—and she wanted to know if there was anyone to call other than the police. I wrote down the phone number for animal control and gave her the Humane Society of the United States' dogfighting fact sheet.

Later, a man locked eyes with me. He crossed the bustling aisle. "Is your dog a pit bull?" he asked. I gave him my spiel about "pit bull" being a generic term. I explained Emmett was a Staffordshire Bull Terrier mix, a therapy dog, and an all-around cuddle bug. The guy told me that, *yeah, yeah, yeah*, he knew pit bulls have an unfair reputation because he had a pit bull, and she was just the best dog he'd ever had. She was great with his kids, and she loved to go for walks or nap on the couch.

"She's so well trained," he bragged. "I can sic her on anything, but now she's killing all my neighborhood's cats. How can I get her to stop killing cats?"

Um. For starters, I thought, stop siccing her on things.

Emmett pranced home after big events like the county fair because, after all, he was the star of the show who was spoiled by his adoring fans—in his mind, anyway. Meanwhile, I dragged myself home after events like that. I struggled to wrap my mind around how people could treat animals so poorly and rest their heads on their pillows at night.

But I had Emmett with me. My solid, furry support system. I had Lucas and Cooper at home.

I relied on my dogs to buoy my spirits. Without fail, I could count on them to wag their tails when they saw me walk in the front door and to snuggle me as I rested after a long day. I relied on my dogs and they relied on me. We worked as a team, no matter what was thrown our way.

Including, as it turned out, other animals.

When John found Molly, the tiny black-and-brown puppy was sprinting across an empty part of the bayou. He stopped his car, whistled, and opened his door. She hesitated but ultimately ran toward him, jumped in the back, twirled around, and fell asleep on the ledge between the back seat and the rearview window. The poor little puppy was exhausted from running for however long she spent in the desolate stretch of swamp. One eye was swollen shut with a crusty infection. Her long, soft fur jumped with fleas.

Though he was on his way to work, John did a U-turn on the highway and drove straight home. He called me to put the dogs and Newt in a separate area so he could bring in the puppy. I took one look at her and called the vet. They squeezed her in later that same day.

"Whoever had her," the vet said, "probably dumped her because of that eye. It's easier and cheaper to find a new dog than it is to treat an infection."

We decided to help her heal and then find her a permanent home. We were at our limit, both spatially and financially, but we wanted to get her on the right path before we found an adopter.

Her eye cleared up after several rounds of medicated cream, though it was heavily scarred. The fleas disappeared with a Capstar dose. She gained weight. She started to settle into our home and routine, though she stayed on leash or separated during mealtimes and playtimes because Molly guarded her food and toys when around the boys. She froze and snarled over each scrap of food. Until one day she didn't. Until one day she began to feel safe.

I kept her leashed until one day Cooper gave her a little play bow and she returned the gesture. I removed Emmett and Lucas from the area—lowering the risk of a fight breaking out—and waited to see what would happen. She played chase with Cooper. The two zipped around and alternated who was the chaser and who was the chasee. It went so well, I began unclipping her leash around the boys whenever toys and food weren't around.

One day she skittered with Lucas, the eighty-pound Shepherd chasing the faster and more agile fifteen-pound puppy.

She adored Emmett, who had zero interest in playing with a puppy, especially one who followed him and worshiped him like an acolyte.

She settled in.

Whatever had happened to her in her short little life, she recovered. And she recovered pretty quickly. It was almost as if she looked around one day and thought, "Oh, wait. This place isn't so bad. This is actually kind of great." More importantly, though, it was safe.

Watching Molly find herself cast our battle with Lucas into a stark light. It took her days to discover her footing. Lucas took so much longer—years and years—to find his confidence. We had been working together so hard for so long that I couldn't take it for granted that a dog like Molly could slip into comfort and safety so easily.

Fight. Flight. Freeze. These reactions to fear aren't done with any foresight. They're not intentional. It's not a conscious decision. "Oh, woah. I'm scared. I'm going to fight this threat." Or, "Uh oh, that guy's bigger than I am. Better run!" It's not planned. It's not thought through. It's just done.

Our dogs—and, for that matter, we humans—prefer to flee. Who wants to get in a fight? Fights are dangerous. You might get hurt! But, dogs aren't fighting just to fight. Most often, dogs choose to fight in response to fear because they're trying to scare the threat away from them. The opposite is true for dogs who flee; they're trying to get the other dog to move away from them.

Lucas chose to fight when out and about. He'd lunge. He'd snarl. He'd growl. He'd bark. Twice, he even attempted to bite a stranger. He wasn't a vicious dog. He wasn't picking a fight for the sake of getting in a fight. He wanted to get the other person or dog away. *Now*. And he tried to achieve his need for safety in the only way he knew how: by scaring the adversary to leave.

The nature versus nurture debate has raged since 1869. That year, psychologist Sir Francis Galton popularized the phrase;

however, genetics versus environment had been debated long before that, just without the catchy phrase. Long, long before Sir Galton, around 400 BCE, Hippocrates described behavior as solely biological. Centuries later, Jean-Jacques Rousseau and John Locke argued behavior was solely environmental—that people were born blank slates ready to be filled in by what happened to them. Between Hippocrates and Locke and Galton and today, the argument waged: What determines who we are? Our biology or our experiences?

These days, most scientists agree it's a bit of both. When I was a college freshman, my biological anthropology professor described it as all of us being an artist's palette. We're born with a specific shape with spaces ready to be filled with paint (genetics). But none of us end up filling a palette with the same colors in the same places (environment), so none of the paintings end up the same (personality).

Our dogs are the same. They're born with a set of genetics that determines a lot about who they are and what they can become, but their experiences heavily impact their personalities, too. Their lives are so short that the cycle of nature versus nurture feels sped up, and it makes those early weeks and months that much more important to their lifelong wellbeing.

I started to consider Lucas's problem behaviors against Cooper's and developed a hypothesis: Lucas's issues stemmed from the "nurture" part of the equation. His "nature" was fun-loving, raucous, and playful. His start to life, fighting for survival on the streets for six months or so, set him up for serious struggles he was able to work on and eventually overcome. All the training, all the walks, all the counterconditioning, all the positive reinforcement, all of it added up to big improvements in his confidence and his behavior. Mostly.

While we never knew any details of the first six to eight months of Lucas's life, it's safe to assume his socialization wasn't great. His environment, the people and animals and experiences he faced, didn't set him up for a lifetime of success. It took years of concentrated hard work to dismantle the impact of his early learning. His nature, though, proved to be funny and fun-loving. Once we chipped away at the guard rails he'd built up as a defensive mechanism, we found a sweet, goofy, charming pup who could make friends with anyone—as long as he felt secure.

Cooper, though, seemed hardwired for anxiety despite a positive puppyhood. His "nature" seemed nervous, high-strung, and fearful. He didn't want to wander away from my side. He didn't want to play independently. He wanted to stay safe. All the same training, walks, conditioning, counterconditioning, and positive reinforcement that helped Lucas improve only made minimal improvements in Cooper's anxious response. Instead of changing his behavior like it did with Lucas, all our training simply taught Cooper—and us—how to manage his fears.

By the time Molly came along, I had already put years of training into Emmett, Lucas, and Cooper. I relied on them to behave in ways that were incredibly predictable due to their unique personalities.

Molly shared characteristics with all three boys, but in different ways. She was a young pup who we assumed had not been treated well; our assumption was based on the simple fact that she was dumped in the middle-of-nowhere bayou covered with fleas and suffering from a raging eye infection. Yet, it only took a few days for her to settle in and get comfy with people and dogs. Cats were a different story—she and Newt and, later, foster kitten Petey, could never be in the same room. Molly was happily adopted into a home without cats but with a big dog sister who was three times Molly's size but had all the same black-and-brown markings. The match felt fated.

Not all dogs land in a home with people who can help them recover from whatever trauma has occurred. Some end up in worse situations and others languish or perish in shelters. Whether it's nature or nurture matters only to the extent that we can use what we know to help dogs recover.

The threads of a behavior tapestry are so intricately woven, we can't separate one single piece of thread from another without the entire design unraveling. Even if nothing bad happened to a dog at the hand of a person, like Cooper, or even if a human did have a hand in mistreatment, like Molly, or even if you have no backstory on why a dog behaves a certain way, like Lucas and Emmett, the reality is the same: It is our job to hold the other end of the leash with calm, compassionate, gentle leadership. Human behavior impacts the wellbeing of animals. To our knowledge, Cooper never had anything bad happen to him, but unscrupulous backyard breeding led to his wonky DNA—his unstable wiring.

Many years ago, during our first stint in Indiana, neighbors reported a woman in the next county over for animal hoarding. There were no social services in place to help her, but twenty-four dogs were removed from her trailer home. Three of the walls of the trailer were intact; the fourth wall crumbled, reinforced by a chain-link fence. The plywood floors were so urine-soaked they squished underfoot.

She got to keep some of her dogs, six or so, though her neighbors said when she found out an animal welfare organization was coming, she ferried even more dogs to a friend's house.

I helped with the twenty-four recovered dogs. Their nails were so long, they curled underneath and into the pads of their feet. Their teeth were rotten or missing, and all suffered from ear infections and fleas. All but one of the dogs were able to be placed in various shelters to await their fate. The one remaining dog had clearly birthed many litters over her long-suffering life and simply couldn't emerge from the fog of fear and ill health.

As for the woman, nothing happened. Not one thing, because there weren't enough resources in that county to help her.

The majority of the dogs could probably recover. There's a chance some ended up like Lucas, scared and skittish of people and defensive around other dogs. But there's a chance that those who ended up like Lucas could recover, at least to an extent. Their innate dogness might allow them to preserve, to recover, to forgive.

Dogs are our partners. They evolved to team up with us. We fail them again and again in ways big and small. And yet they always come back to us, because we are programmed by tens of thousands of years of evolution to be partners.

I strive to not fail my dogs, my most reliable partners.

During our two-year stint in southern Louisiana, our pack swelled to include Molly, who we ultimately transported back to Indiana for adoption since we couldn't find a good home for her in Houma, and Petey, the gray kitten John spotted stuck in the middle of the highway. Before we left for Indiana, a coworker from John's lab decided to adopt Petey because his longtime cat had recently passed away and he was looking for a little buddy.

But before that, before we found them homes, we needed to get them well. And caring for a puppy and a kitten on top of our three dogs and cat required juggling. More than juggling, actually. It was a three-ring circus.

With our four animals—Emmett, Lucas, Cooper, and Newt—plus the two strays, I established a solid routine that allowed me to feed everyone, to keep them all safe, and to get my work done. It was a reliable, repeatable routine.

Until John traveled out of town for work.

I knew it wouldn't be easy—"survival mode" is what I called it—but I didn't want to let the dogs and cats down, either, just because it was a lot to manage. I wanted to be as reliable for them as they were for me.

I could easily rotate Emmett, Lucas, and Cooper, because they could be around Molly, Newt, and Petey; however, Petey couldn't be around Newt, and Molly couldn't be around Petey or Newt, so I tried to figure out how to divide my time and attention. After days of pouring rain, we were all stir-crazy, and I had barely spent any time with Petey because the dogs were under-exercised and simply needed more of me than the kitten in our upstairs bathroom.

So, when I got scheduled on a conference call, I did what any normal—*Can we still use the word "normal" in this house?* I wondered—person would do and took my long morning call in the bathroom with the kitten. No barking dogs. No switching anyone around. Plus, playing and helping Petey socialize.

I set up my laptop, grabbed my notebook, pulled out some cat toys, and logged into my conference—with the video camera turned off. Petey climbed all over my lap, up my arms, onto my shoulders. She chewed my hair, chased my typing fingers, pounced on the toys I tossed, and enjoyed herself immensely.

About thirty minutes into the call, she popped down off her perch on my shoulder, toddled over to her box, climbed in, and at that moment I learned Petey had an upset stomach.

She was miniscule—only about one pound at this point—and clumsy. She hadn't yet figured out where her legs were in space. When she tried to bury her business on a normal day, she covered herself and the bathroom in litter. I'd check on her every few hours, and each time, I brushed litter off her and swept litter off the floor.

With severe GI distress, she kicked and scratched and buried. Not only was the litter scattered all around the bathroom, but all her diarrhea splattered everywhere. Most of her body was covered in it, as well as the wall and surrounding cabinet. The smell filled the small, enclosed space. I gagged and started to get up to turn on the fan, but at that precise moment, my section of the call began.

I took a deep breath with my nose tucked into my T-shirt. I unmuted and began my presentation. As I spoke, I realized with horror that Petey was ready to play. She wobbled straight toward me.

I couldn't do anything to stop her as I clicked through my slides, giving my brief talk. Petey climbed straight up my legs, clawed her way up my arm, and perched onto my shoulder, her favorite spot to hang out. My clothing was soiled, my arm was scratched, but somehow my voice never cracked.

I finished the call. Swept up the litter crumbs. Put her back in her box. She curled up in a little ball, exhausted from her long play and potty session. At least I achieved a bit of socialization for her.

Since I had to walk from the upstairs bathroom through the rest of the house, past all the dogs and Newt covered in potentially disease-ridden and definitely worm-ridden fecal matter, I stripped, held my clothes above my head, and made it across the house in my undies. I ducked outside and into the garage where our washer and dryer were, stuffed the clothes in, and started the wash.

If only this were the first time I was out here in my underwear, I thought as I yanked the back door open and scuttled inside to shower.

But it wasn't.

The first time started like every other day. With six animals in the house, many of whom couldn't be around the others safely, I needed the solidity of a daily routine. John left for work early. I took care of all the animal chores, worked, and exercised. As evening fell, I took care of all the animal chores again, worked some more, then fell into bed exhausted. John usually arrived home later—in time for us to eat dinner—and would help shift animals around. They were long days but structured. Routinized.

The morning routine was the easiest: I scooped the two cats' litter boxes, and Petey stayed in her bathroom. Newt went behind the upstairs gate. All four dogs ate, then followed me into the office to take naps or chew on toys.

I took a long lunch hour each day to swap all the animals around—Emmett and Lucas walked together first, then Molly walked with Cooper, then Molly went into her crate. I let Newt out downstairs while Molly was crated, and let Petey out of her bathroom upstairs in the office to play with Cooper. Emmett and Lucas rotated between Newt downstairs and Cooper and Petey upstairs. Every day, I ate lunch at my desk while completing my admin tasks like emails and invoices to make up for the long midday break.

Most mornings, I squeezed in a ten-minute workout video once the animals were all settled after breakfast because afternoons were such chaos. Between the dog walks and the short workout each day, I was slowly rebuilding my strength after cancer and chemo, but I had a long way to go.

That day, I tried a kickboxing video. I'm clumsy and uncoordinated and couldn't figure out the moves. I spent the first five minutes trying to get my legs to do what the instructors were doing, and I simply couldn't. I quit. I turned it off and went downstairs to pour a glass of water.

When I got back upstairs with my glass of water, I spotted Lucas in the hunched-over-heaving-back position all dog lovers know.

Lucas threw up regularly. It was a symptom of his anxiety, so John and I were used to spotting it coming and mitigating the disaster. Somehow he always aimed for carpet or rugs, never wood or tile, so I executed the maneuver John and I perfected over the years: I whipped off my T-shirt and caught the puke. It's so much easier to launder a single shirt than shampoo a carpet.

I gathered the shirt and turned to hustle him straight outside. Lucas always puked two times in a row, and the laundry was in the garage, so I wanted to try to get him out before he barfed again. As I turned to usher him along, I saw Molly squat in the other position. The first little poop hit the carpet, so I used the sleeve of my barf shirt to pick it up. I snatched up Molly in my other hand and bellowed, "Outside!"

I rushed the dogs out, dropped the little poop from the shirt into the yard, shook out the vomit, and tossed the shirt into the washing machine. I ran back into the yard to see if Lucas had hurled again or if Molly had finished pooping. I stood in the middle of the yard, watching Lucas puke and Molly poop, and I realized, yep, I stood in our yard without a shirt on.

It's no wonder all our neighbors avoided us.

Even though the dogs who have come into my life have been pets, never intended to herd or hunt, we naturally partnered up to get through life. We walked together. We cuddled on the couch. We curled up and slept side by side. We played and ran and worked as a team. As a result, they nurtured the person I was into the person I am. A person who ends up outside in the yard—twice—without all her clothes on.

My nature is what it is. I was born a shy introvert. I love to make wisecracks. I prefer quiet to loud. I have a weakness for salt and vinegar potato chips. I escape into books and writing because I'm most comfortable in my head, lost in a world of words. Those are things I was born with.

Dogs, though, nurtured my life. They've taught me resilience by example. They've shown me what it means to experience unbridled joy and what it means to give in wholly to rest.

Everyone is doing their best. Everyone is trying their best with what they have. But sometimes someone's best simply isn't good enough. Thankfully, as humans, we have the self-awareness and capacity to identify these flaws about ourselves. It's not easy, but we have the ability.

Our dogs? Well, they probably don't have the same self-awareness that we have. In fact, most other animals don't. It's a uniquely human thing; it's also uniquely human that we can ignore our best interests and keep making one bad decision after another.

For all they gave back to me, though, all of it—even the outside-in-my-underwear embarrassments—fulfilled a much greater purpose. In a tables-turned kind of way, our dogs serve as our therapists by helping us become more resilient and protecting us against the effects of stress and illness.

Not everyone would go to the same lengths we did to care for Molly and Petey, or even Newt, Emmett, Lucas, and Cooper. Others might have had the resources to provide extravagant care that didn't involve vomit-stained T-shirts. But we did our best with what we had.

Because of dogs—and not just my own—I've changed over the years. I'm not the same person I would've been if I hadn't grown up with my childhood dogs, Sparky or Lennon or Rutherford. I'm not the same as I would've been if Emmett hadn't launched into my lap and changed the fabric of my life. He taught me unconditional love and the power of outreach. He taught me how to use my voice, even if it's uncomfortable. I'm not the same person I would've been if Lucas hadn't taught me about compassion and patience. I'm definitely not the same as I would've been without Cooper squeaking his way into my heart and attaching himself permanently to my ankle, showing me the healing power of safety and security.

I might've learned those things some other way. I might've become somewhat like who I am today. But I wouldn't be this person without dogs, and that is both humbling and inspiring. Imagine how much your world could change if you opened your heart up to an animal. Maybe it already has. Maybe you know exactly what I'm talking about. Maybe you can look down at your feet right now and see the furry head of a dog who has changed your very existence. I sure hope so, because it's the most wonderful feeling in the world to have the love of a good dog—and they are all good dogs.

CHAPTER 7

Kind Hearts and Wagging Tails

During a warm stretch of early spring, I crouched under the draped limbs of a leafy mulberry tree. That year, no mulberries grew, but we used the shade created by the overhang to build a perennial shade garden Violet dubbed our secret garden. I pulled the weeds crowding out the base of the tree and the plugs of grass creeping in around my flowers.

While I filled a bucket, three-year-old Violet tootled around the yard. She collected the shed shells of cicadas and stuffed them into her pockets. As John walked toward my garden spot, I was poised to ask him to remind me to empty the spent bug shells before I ran the laundry later, but the expression on his face stopped me.

He ducked under the mulberry branches. "Otto died. He had a stroke last night, and he died." Tears pooled in the corners of his eyes.

Otto, my mom's beloved dog. We spent countless hours, days, and weeks dog-sitting Otto over the thirteen years of his charmed life. He met Lucas when Otto was a tiny puppy, and the two became instant best friends. They grew up playing tug-of-war and snuggling on a shared dog bed. Lucas—at eighty pounds—felt safe and secure playing with Otto—at twenty pounds—and Otto's outsized personality matched Lucas's physical size. They played together perfectly.

I knew Otto was aging, and I knew he had health problems, but I wasn't ready for him to die. John's news took me off guard, and my eyes burned with tears. The suddenness filled my stomach with lead. Little Otto. How we all loved him.

Violet wandered over. John and I locked eyes and held an unspoken conversation: *Do we tell her now or wait to find the right words? Now. It has to be now.*

The summer before, Violet's betta fish, Taco Fish, died after a couple days of not eating and floating listlessly at the bottom of his tank. During those two days, we created a narrative around TF getting sick and aging because we knew he didn't have much time left, and we wanted to prepare her for her first loss.

On the day he actually died, she came downstairs after her nap. "We have some sad news," I said. "Taco Fish died while you were napping."

She ran to his tank and peered in. "Where is he?" she asked.

"He's no longer in there, sweetie. He died. He's gone," I said.

"No, no, no," she said. "Where's his body? Where did you put Taco Fish?"

We had put him in a box in the fridge so we could hold a fish funeral for him, and Violet insisted upon seeing his body. After she looked and realized his gills weren't moving, that he couldn't swim anymore, she broke down. She flung herself onto Cooper's dog bed and sobbed big, heaving tears.

"I love him so much," she cried. "Why did he die? I miss him."

Later, we sat around the kitchen table, and we discussed with Violet how she wanted to hold a funeral for Taco Fish in the backyard. She wanted a rock to mark his burial site, and she wanted to sing him a song.

"Mama." Her eyes turned serious. "Mama, will Taco Fish go to heaven?"

"Oh, Violet. Yes. Of course. Taco Fish is in heaven."

"No, he's not. He's in a box in the fridge," she said.

We buried Taco Fish in the corner of Violet's fairy garden. After his funeral, she dragged her blue plastic toddler-sized patio chair over to his gravesite and sat down. "I want to keep an eye on him," she said. "I want to be alone." We left her there until she was ready to come inside.

The rest of the day and into the next morning, she periodically asked questions: *What happens when you die? Where do you go? Do you still breathe?* We did our best to answer them all, and as Violet walked toward us the day Otto died, I thought through all those questions and wondered how she'd react.

"Violet," I said. "We have some sad news."

She froze in place. "What? Why are you crying?"

"Otto died last night."

She looked into my face. Took a few deep breaths. Then she said, "We should go to the pet store right now and adopt a dog for Grandma and Grandpa so they won't be sad anymore."

Of course, any pet lover can tell you a new dog or cat never replaces the one who passed away. The time and the habits and the routines built over many years of pet ownership can't be filled, at least not for a while. If you had set your alarm for 5:00 a.m. for the last ten years to walk your dog an hour before work, suddenly sleeping in feels devastating. Adding a new dog to the family doesn't replace the lost dog. It simply allows your body and your heart to continue taking that walk every morning. It makes sense to a degree: We grieve the loss of a pet so profoundly that adding a new one seems, on the surface, a way to fill the void.

In a study that looked at subjective happiness against two life events—the acquisition of and the death of a pet—researchers reported "those who felt most negatively about the loss of their pet were most eager to obtain a new one."

"Dogs are not our whole life, but they make our lives whole," Roger Caras once said.

What does it mean for us as humans to love dogs so fully?

What does it mean to dedicate your time, your energy, and your money to a creature destined to die too soon? Why do we cast our lots with these animals, invite them into our homes and under our blankets, knowing full well we will say goodbye again and again and again?

We dog lovers adopt a dog or purchase a puppy, knowing the instant we fall in love, we will eventually say goodbye. Their timelines are so compressed, so short. An entire lifetime occurs in about a decade. We start out with a little seed of grief already planted in our hearts. This delightful ball of fluff and fuzz and mischief will be an old man in a handful of years. Then, this best friend who has shared every moment, every high and low, leaves us.

Why do we do this to ourselves over and over again?

We pay for a lifetime of joy with immense grief. We trade a decade or so of our lives, caring for and loving and needing our dog, for a heart-shattering goodbye.

It would be easier to say, "No more dogs. I can't take this pain anymore." It would be easier to donate all the leashes and bowls to the animal shelter, to wash the dog bed and drop it off for a friend's new puppy. It would be easier to fill that early morning walk with an extra hour of sleep, to not worry about rushing home from work to let her out, to put all the money from vet visits toward a family vacation.

Sure. Of course. It absolutely would be easier.

But would a life without dogs be worthwhile?

John and I sat in the lobby of the veterinary teaching hospital waiting for Emmett to finish his round of checkups and exams. We heard an elderly couple who sat across from us express their fears of administering an oral chemo at home to their dog, Dixie. Their concerns centered around one theme: What if something goes wrong?

We heard them tell the oncology resident about Dixie, about how she literally saved their lives from a burglar and how she, as his farmhand, once saved him from a charging bull.

We heard them explain how she was their baby, how their kids were grown, how she was everything to them.

With all that we had been through recently, listening to their story tore at our hearts. When the resident walked away, without hesitating or rehearsing what I wanted to say, I jumped in and introduced myself and John. We explained that Emmett took an oral chemo for over a year, and we shared our experience: how we safely stored the medication (fridge), how we handled it (gloves), how he responded (perfectly, thank goodness). They asked us how we got him to take the pills because, they told us, Dixie was picky about pills. We told them we gave Em his worst one shoved inside a large marshmallow every day. They asked us if we subscribed to a veterinary journal about cancer. We didn't, but they said it was invaluable and pulled out a file with marked-up, highlighted articles. We chatted some more and discovered, coincidently, they lived near us. Before we both were called into exam rooms, they asked for our address so they could send us information about that veterinary journal.

Our appointments ended at the same time, and we parted ways at the checkout.

A few days later, John went out to collect the mail and came back with a photocopy of the latest issue of the journal along with a note and a reply card so we could mail it in to start a subscription.

That gesture—the couple going through the effort of photocopying the magazine, then driving it to our home with a reply card—perfectly reflects the tremendous kindness that accompanies cancer. And dog people.

One night, after we put the girls to bed, John and I turned on a movie. The cats climbed on my lap. Cooper settled onto the blanket between us. John patted Cooper and rubbed his ears.

"Oh, no," he said. He turned Coop's collar this way and that. "His tags are gone."

Not a big deal, really, since our county didn't require a license tag. We were just missing his name tag and rabies tag. In my head, I was already trying to fit in a trip to the pet store to have a new tag made while I ran errands the next day. I could call the vet to request a copy of his rabies certificate to scan and store in my phone, just in case. It would take an hour or so out of my week—a little annoying, but not bad.

The next afternoon, I walked down the driveway to retrieve the mail. When I opened the box, Coop's tags were sitting on top of our bills and magazines.

"John!" I ran into the house. "Someone picked up Cooper's tags and brought them to our house. They were in the mailbox."

There wasn't a note or card, but we were so grateful for that person's generosity. It was such a kind thing to do, especially because the tags could've fallen off anywhere around town; John and Coop had run half a dozen miles together the day before.

I'm a sucker for random acts of kindness. I cry over Facebook videos of people paying it forward in the drive-through line and teachers finding their cars washed by their students. I sob—a big, huge ugly-cry—at dogs being reunited with their owners after being found by a good Samaritan. And I tear up at the memes of the elderly gentleman bringing the bag of tennis balls to the animal shelter or the kids giving free biscuits at their lemonade stands. I love kindness.

As an in-recovery people pleaser, I enjoy doling out kindness more than receiving it. When people do nice things for me, I feel awkward and uncomfortable. It takes a lot for me to ask for help.

I've noticed, though, that dogs ask for help all the time. If only we paid them more attention when they ask.

Lucas used to play with toys by himself when he couldn't rally Emmett or Cooper. He'd toss a ball or rope, chase it down, thrash it around, then throw it again. Often, the toy would land somewhere he couldn't reach: under the couch, on top of the bookcase, on the kitchen table. He'd dash over to me and stare. As soon as I looked at him, he'd rush over to the area where the toy was lost and look back at me. He waited for me to follow and retrieve it for him, which I always did.

I've seen dogs do kind acts for others—everyone has. They're in the news almost daily. The dog who pulled a toddler out of a burning home. The dog who kept the lost little girl warm until rescuers found her deep in the woods. The dog who led pedestrians walking down the sidewalk to a litter of kittens abandoned under a house. These stories are filmed on cell phones, posted on social media, and quickly go viral because we all can relate. We know what it feels like. We know this relationship. Dogs do great things.

None of those things happened because the dog was trained to do it. And for dogs who are trained in service, they often go above and beyond what's expected of them to help the people they serve.

But is this kindness? Can they extend generosity to those in need in a purposeful way? Or are all these dogs who do kind things for others doing it out of some inborn instinct?

During my year of chemo, especially while John lived in Louisiana and I was in Indiana, people did incredibly kind things, even when it was difficult. At the same time, my dogs changed their behavior, too, like how they adjusted their sleeping positions to help me stay warm or to cool down. Were they responding to my ambient temperature? Probably. But did they have to move? Nope. They chose to.

Do our dogs have the capacity for kindness? I can unequivocally say yes.

My dogs are better friends than I am. Sometimes it takes me two weeks to reply to a text because I'm distracted or tired. I never answer my phone, unless it's my mother, but I can say with total certainty that if our dogs could text or answer the phone, they'd do so immediately, each and every time we reached out.

My dogs are always here and ready to cuddle or play or walk or doze with me. Whatever I need, whenever I need it. I'd spend every minute of every day with Coop by my side if I could. Of course, he would hate that because he wants to be home more than anywhere else and would be a nervous wreck if he had to run errands with me, but the big difference is that—if he wanted to—I'd enjoy his company all day long, whereas I'd rather John find something else to do than go to Target or Petco with me. When I go into my head, when I read my book, when I settle in for quiet time at night after the girls fall asleep, I want Cooper by my side.

We welcome our dogs into our quiet places, into our privacy. There's never been a point in my life when I wanted my dogs to go away. In fact, it's often the opposite. After a hard day, a failed test, tripping in front of Panera and spilling all our takeout into the shrubbery, whatever, dogs are there without judgment. Their generosity is their presence. Can our dogs tell when we're sad? When we need some extra love? When we're bursting with joy? Research says yes.

But just because someone—person or pet—can tell what kind of mood we're in doesn't necessarily mean they'll react in a kind or generous way. One thing doesn't always lead to the other.

So, when Emmett cuddled the little girl crying in the hallway, or when Lucas got excited as I jumped around the room after my last chemo shot, or when Cooper allowed toddler Violet to rest her head on his back, they were not just acting out of instinct. It's not instinctual to comfort or support someone, especially not of another species. Yet, they do. Time and time again, dogs extend an incredible gift of, yeah, kindness.

Of course, attributing an abstract concept like kindness might border on anthropomorphizing. However, research shows dogs do have the capacity for kindness. Maybe what's most astounding is how they're willing to bestow it upon us when we oftentimes don't deserve it.

In a *Time* special publication dedicated to dogs, reporter Jeffrey Kluger explained how our unlikely friendship with dogs occurred by genetic coincidence. He wrote:

> It was only by the tiniest bit of genetic chance that our cross-species union was forged at all. Dogs and wolves share 99.9% of their mitochondrial DNA—the DNA that's passed down by the mother alone—which makes the two species nearly indistinguishable. But elsewhere in the genome, there are a few genetic scraps that make a powerful difference. On chromosome six in particular, investigators have found three genes that code for hyper-sociability—and they are in the same spot as similar genes linked to similar sweetness in humans.

Most people can spend time around dogs, even unknown dogs, and know how the dog is feeling. By a certain bark, by observing facial expressions and body language, most people can make a fair assumption about how a dog is feeling, and it's usually pretty accurate. This is a big part of how special our relationship with dogs is. In the *Time* article, Kluger writes, "Think that's not a big deal? Then answer this: What does a happy bird look like? A sad lion? You don't know, but dog talk you get."

Even if our dogs don't understand the concept of kindness, they sure do know how we're feeling, and we know how they're feeling. A reciprocal relationship relies on prosocial behavior—or, helpful, positive behavior that promotes social wellbeing. It relies on us being nice to dogs since dogs are genetically inclined to be nice to us.

When I first started chemo, the cancer center was far from our house—about ninety minutes one way—but only fifteen minutes from my parents' house. So, John and I, and Emmett, Lucas, and Cooper relocated to their house until we got our bearings.

Every single day, after I had my infusion, I returned to my childhood bedroom and curled up in bed to sleep off the worst of the nausea. Cooper stopped whatever he was doing, followed me up to bed, and laid on top of the comforter at my feet. Sometimes he slept, but mostly he watched me. Every time I opened my eyes, I saw him angled at my feet so he could look up at my face. Cooper was my guardian. He made me feel warm and secure when I was sicker than sick. Someone would have to come and physically get him to go to the bathroom or to eat dinner because he only wanted to be with me. For the first few days, he even growled at anyone other than John who tried to bring me tea or medicine.

Our shared experience during that time bonded us more than I could have imagined. Since then, Cooper rarely moves from my side. The entirety of this book will likely be composed with him asleep under my desk.

His steadfastness was the greatest kindness anyone, dog or human, could have extended to me during the most difficult time of my life. Even the people who loved me couldn't stay in my room and watch me at all hours, nor did I want them to. But Cooper could, and he did, without wavering and without—as far as I could tell—any resentment for missing out on playtime with Emmett and Lucas.

I've witnessed dogs being gentle: Emmett and Lucas allowed puppy Cooper to learn the ropes and even let him play with toys they typically didn't share.

I've witnessed dogs asking for kindness: When John and I were in Guatemala for a friend's wedding, dogs wandered up and asked for pets and eyed us hopefully for food.

I've witnessed generosity: The boys letting foster puppy Molly chew a special antler.

Of course, I've also witnessed the other side. The fights. The aggression. The bared teeth and snarling. The biting.

Oftentimes, in discussions around dogs' capacity for emotion or specific behaviors generally attributed to humans, people who aren't familiar with the research cite dog fights and resource guarding, aggression, and dog bites.

If a dog can bite a kid, the argument goes, *how can they possibly be kind? They're just animals. Deep down, they're savage.*

Humans have a great capacity for kindness. People often reach out to help others, like the couple who passed along the canine cancer journal. People are kind even to those they've never met, like the person who returned Cooper's tags.

But humans can also be horrible to one another. It wouldn't be fair to judge the generosity of our spirit by the few who treat others terribly.

For many dogs who guard their food and toys, or lash out at other dogs or even people, it's not a matter of whether or not they're capable of kindness. More likely, their behavior is the result of mistreatment, lack of training, or lack of socialization.

The same can be said for people who abuse others.

Among humans, the drive to help each other out is called "other-regarding," and we people have an other-regarding preference. We prefer to be helpful, to help one another. Researchers in Austria wondered if dogs did, too.

They set up an experiment where dogs were trained to pull one of two levers: one gave a treat to another dog and one gave nothing to the other dog. The puller dog got nothing in either scenario. The question was simple: Would the puller dog give treats to another dog without any rewards or motivations for himself?

The authors reported it was rare for a dog to pull the empty tray. They most often gave each other treats, and when the pair of dogs knew each other, the rate of treat-giving went up even higher. The authors concluded that their experiment showed, yes, dogs are other-regarding.

The dogs didn't *have* to dole out any treats—and some didn't, though most did. The study authors suggest this prosocial behavior evolved among dogs because they relied so heavily on cooperative behavior for survival.

Just like humans.

The kids Emmett and I worked with at the mental health facility experienced extreme unkindness. Once, we arrived at the hospital super early. Our usual kids weren't in the gym yet, so we hung out with some little girls in the waiting room. They patted Emmett, rubbed his belly, got high fives, and squashed him with big bear hugs.

A tiny girl, no more than six but small for her age, sauntered over in bare feet and a dress long outgrown. She threw her arms around Emmett's neck. "He's so sweet!" She pushed a clump of tangled hair out of her eyes and looked up at me. Her fingers twined through his fur. She twisted her lips into a snarl and tilted her head. "Until he turns on you."

Her expression was too cynical and too sinister for a child so little. I crouched down to her eye level and smiled softly. "Emmett would never turn on you or anyone. He's friendly. He's well trained, he's a therapy dog, he loves people, and he's well socialized. You can feel safe," I said. I rubbed Em on the top of his head. "He's a really good dog."

"Well, my dog was really good, but one day she bit my fingers so my dad hit her head with a hammer so she died."

At that moment, I wished with my whole entire being I knew the right response to give that little girl. But I didn't. All I could say was how sorry I was that that had happened to her. Within a minute or two, we were paged to head back for our pet therapy session, and I staggered away, gripping Emmett's leash and steadying my breathing before we had to work.

Over the years we worked at the facility, we heard numerous stories of parents, siblings, and friends killing animals, sometimes for no reason other than, "Our Chihuahua had too many puppies." Or, "He was mad."

Those kiddos weren't without problems. We wouldn't have been working with them if they were. But they showed resilience at every single visit. They worked with me to teach Emmett new tricks—although, as I mentioned earlier, I taught him everything in advance so the kids would never fail. They worked together to create an obstacle course for him to run. One day they spent an entire hour taking turns throwing Rupert, Emmett's favorite stuffed squeaky bear, and cheering every time he chased it down. The only reason they stopped after an hour was because Emmett stopped. He was too exhausted to keep chasing Rupert.

Years after Emmett's retirement from therapy dog work, John and I got to visit with one of the counselors and her husband. They invited us to their farm to see their chickens and dogs.

"The kids used to draw pictures of Emmett," she said. "They talked about him all the time in between visits."

When we returned home, I cuddled Em on his dog bed and told him his friends thought of him often. I rubbed his silky ears and felt a deep longing to turn back the years, to make him young again. "You changed lives, guy," I said as he fell asleep with his chin on my lap.

All those years, all those acts of kindness.

Whether or not Emmett thought of them as kind never mattered. His outgoing, friendly, steady nature played a huge part, but he also singled out the kid who needed him the most time and time again. I watched boys and girls argue over who got to pet him first or play intense rounds of paper-rock-scissors to see who could throw his toy first, and he'd wait patiently, look around at all the kids, and saunter over to one—seemingly at random—and that kid would almost always burst into tears. Or, he'd pick out one quiet kid to sit by, and the kid would whisper into his ears as he'd wag his tail.

"Can Emmett keep a secret?" a little girl once asked me in earnest. Her brows furrowed while she watched my face for the answer.

"Emmett is an excellent secret-keeper," I said. "In fact, he's never spilled one single secret ever."

She nodded. It was the answer she was hoping for.

She trotted over to Emmett, bent down, put her face right up to his ear, and started whispering. Emmett, to my eternal gratitude, sat up straight and listened intently.

"Okay," she said with a curt nod. "He knows my secret." She turned back. "Don't tell, Emmett."

He never did.

CHAPTER 8

Bouncing Back: The Resilience of Dogs

Throughout the Polar Vortex winter, we played with the boys in the basement. Outside, sheets of ice encased our yard, and snow fell inch by inch. The cold settled in and froze our pipes, not once but twice. The concrete slab basement floor felt like a frozen pond under our feet. John and I bundled up and made the most of it. We arranged obstacle courses for the dogs: jump over this broom balanced across these chairs, run under this blanket tunnel, weave through these couch cushions, then pop up onto the futon. Or, we'd grab a pile of tennis balls and toss them every which way, each dog dashing after one right after another.

It burned their energy, kept us from getting stir-crazy, and allowed them to run and jump and play since we couldn't be outside safely. We also booked them at doggy daycare a couple times a week: Lucas and Cooper went together once a week, Cooper went alone a second time, and aging Emmett never went and instead enjoyed extra naps on the days his brothers were gone.

One day, the boys skidded around, wrestling, clobbering each other, and chasing tennis balls. In the midst of the game, Lucas yelped. He held up his front left leg. He placed it down and limped across the room.

We ended the game and brought the dogs upstairs. Lucas behaved like a WWE champ on the cold, hard concrete, and he had been at daycare the day before, so we figured he probably overdid it. Maybe he hit the slab with too much force chasing down a tennis ball.

The next day, no limp.

A few days later, a limp.

Lucas never allowed injuries to get him down. He'd run full throttle through the pain if we let him. I would never let him, of course. Instead, I scheduled an appointment to have his leg looked at.

The day of his exam, I took all the usual vet-visit precautions: a well-fitted harness, a can of cheese, some cookies. He behaved impeccably. The dog who, early on, required a separate entrance to the vet now sailed through the wait in the lobby, the exam, and the X-rays the vet ordered out of an abundance of caution. The vet and the techs who treated him for years commented on his good behavior.

I sat with him in the lobby while we waited for the vet to go over his X-rays. I gushed over him. "Oh, what a good boy you are," I whispered. I rubbed his ears. "I'm so proud of you! My special little guy! You did amazing!"

The door to the exam room opened and his vet stepped into the lobby. I looked up and saw tears line her eyes.

"This isn't what I expected," she said.

She showed me the X-rays. His bone looked like spider webs. He must've been in intense pain. *How could he hide this?*

"Osteosarcoma," she said. "I'm so sorry."

I knew enough about cancer to know osteosarcoma was one of the bad ones. One of the ones you don't bounce back from. Two dogs, my heart and my soul, both with terminal cancer.

His vet referred us to an oncologist at Purdue University, where we were already established as oncology patients with Em. Now, in addition to Emmett's oncology appointments and my own, I'd be juggling Lucas's. I thought through the logistics: Could I take them together? Would Lucas need chemo, too? What kind of surgery are we looking at? He needed to be seen as soon as we could possibly find an opening. Our vet made a call, and he was immediately put on the schedule.

Why is this happening? We felt so safe.

Nothing is ever safe.

What does it mean to feel safe?

No one, no person or animal, can feel safe without first taking care of security. Security requires adequate food, water, shelter, and freedom from harm. But any of us, animals included, can have those things and still feel unsafe.

One of the ways I know I'm feeling unsafe is by my body's reaction. We know the responses to fear—fight, flight, or freeze—but then there's also the less-measurable version I experience. My body gets hot while, at the same time, my stomach fills with ice. My throat dries up. My heart rate rises. My face burns red. My hands get clammy. When I feel those things, I know the underlying feeling is fear. I feel unsafe. My body gets ready to fight or flee or freeze. Though usually it's a matter of me taking a bunch of deep, steadying breaths, and instead of conquering those feelings, shoving them really far down so I can hold my chin up and speak to a crowd, or whatever. (I realize that may not be the healthiest strategy, but it's the best I've got for now.) When I feel unsafe, I'm rarely ever *actually* unsafe. It's usually made up in my mind. Like public speaking. Or super long lines at a crowded grocery store. Those stressors send my body into anxious overdrive. Am I actually safe? Sure. Public speaking and big crowds aren't going to kill me. But do I *feel* safe? Nope. Not at all. That's why my body has all those sensations.

There's a big, big difference between *being* safe and *feeling* safe.

There are a lot of people who take the opposite tack from me. They're the people who race motorcycles or jump out of airplanes or gamble in New Jersey. They feel safe without actually being safe. They put themselves in risky positions but don't have the fear response many of us do.

Just like people—who fall on a spectrum between panicking about finding a parking space at the grocery store to jumping out of a helicopter with skis strapped to our feet—our dogs have different thresholds for fear, too. And our job is to help our dogs feel safe, so we need to understand their thresholds.

Emmett feared nothing. It wasn't fearlessness like jumping off a cliff for fun, but more in the sense that it never occurred to him to be scared. It never occurred to him that there was anything in life to be feared. He trusted everything and everyone and had such a positive outlook on life that fear never crept in.

Lucas feared everything, at least for a while. When Lucas confronted something fearful, which was often, he lashed out. He lunged. He snarled. He barked. He turned into a pretty scary thing himself. Enmeshed in the fight response, his goal was to scare away the threat before anything could happen. I imagine his mindset was, "If I act all wild and scary, this thing I'm terrified of will leave before anything really bad can happen to me."

Holding the other end of his leash was exhausting.

Trying to desensitize him to myriad everyday things he feared was exhausting.

Counterconditioning the many fears that gripped his mind and transforming them from terrifying to neutral to good was exhausting.

We could never fully alter how his brain worked, of course, so helping Lucas feel safe became the key. Management became our survival mode: keep the front blinds down so he couldn't flip out over things going past our house, tote a can of spray cheese with us everywhere to use as a distraction, walk in bad weather or off-peak times, know our routes, and know where every dog in the neighborhood lived. We scheduled his veterinary exams for weird times by asking the front desk staff for the quietest appointments of the day, and called from the parking lot to let them know we'd arrived to allow them ample time to move the other dogs away from the main entrance.

It was on us to learn his triggers, anticipate the unexpected, and have plans in place at all times to mitigate triggers. Often, though, despite our very best efforts, we failed. Sometimes spectacularly.

One drizzly spring morning shortly before his diagnosis, Lucas and I crested the hill along the east side of the park. I spotted a woman heading toward us on the opposite side of the green. I noted her location but didn't adjust Lucas because single women walking down the street never bothered him. Just things with wheels, men, or anyone with a dog. Especially a man with a dog.

We neared the intersection of her path and ours, and I moved Lucas to my other side, furthest from the woman. Whenever I'm out walking, I smile and nod at anyone I pass, but as we drew closer, the woman stared ahead, swung her arms, and maintained her pace. As we passed each other, Lucas lunged across the front of my body and jumped on the woman. I pulled him back, and he snapped his teeth.

I stopped breathing. My mind went blank.

"Your dog tried to bite me." She spit the words.

My hands shook. I tried to breathe again but could only garble out a slew of confused words. "I'm so sorry. Did he get you? Are you okay? He's never done that before. I'm so, so sorry. Are you hurt?"

She brushed the leg of her jeans, checking for holes.

"Are you okay?" I asked again. Tears pooled behind my eyes. She glared at me. Lucas stood at my side doing absolutely nothing. Calm. Still. Like nothing happened.

She berated me, as she should have. My dog tried to bite her. As she yelled, I nodded and nodded, but I heard none of her tirade because the blood rushing through my ears kept the words from sinking in. I apologized over and over. She pointed to the knee of her jeans, to a tiny hole, and I offered to buy her a new pair.

She strode off.

For a split second I didn't know what to do. My initial fear reaction kicked in and I froze. Stuck in place, all I wanted was to go home and crawl under my covers and sob, but I worried she'd go in the same direction, see where we lived, call the police, send animal control to our door, and have Lucas put down. I'd never seen her before—and I walked the area three times a day most days—so I prayed we'd never cross paths again. Frozen in place, I didn't know which way to turn.

Suddenly, fury flooded my body. My vision blurred with tears—not from sadness, but rage. I yanked on the leash harder than I wished I'd done, turned, and fled. I sprinted us as fast as I could the long way around the park and down the back alley toward our garage to ensure we wouldn't encounter the woman—or anyone else. I punched in the code to our garage door with shaky fingers and barreled underneath the second it rose enough to pull Lucas through. I slammed into the house, unhooked his leash, sat on the floor, and wept.

Years. I had been training with him for years. How could this have happened?

When we adopted Lucas, the shelter listed him as a year old. Within a few months, we knew they overestimated; he was closer to seven or eight months. Regardless, he spent the first part of his life as a stray; he was unsocialized to humans and human things. He felt unsafe around other dogs. In fact, he felt unsafe almost all of the time. In the several years between adopting him and this horrifying incident, Lucas and I took every dog training class I could fit into my budget and schedule. I read piles of books, subscribed to blogs, collected tips and tricks for working with fearful, reactive dogs. I listened to podcasts and watched YouTube videos. I turned this work into my freelance career and interviewed experts, veterinarians, behaviorists. I worked so hard. We made so much progress. And now this.

I thought we were safe.

Nothing is ever safe.

And now, with his terminal diagnosis, I faced the reality of taking him to different animal hospitals, different specialists, different doctors. He could do it, I knew. It was on me to do better by him. I needed to keep him safe.

"You chose to amputate the leg." The oncology resident nodded while she flipped through his chart. "It's not an easy decision but, I think, the right one."

It wasn't a difficult decision for me.

Once we arrived with Lucas at Purdue, the oncology team provided a clearer sense of what we faced. Without amputation, this insidious cancer would take Lucas in only a few weeks. With amputation, his prognosis expanded to half a year. With amputation plus chemo, 50 percent of dogs make it a full year and 25 percent survive for two years.

I looked at the odds, and I looked at Lucas, and I knew. We'd amputate. We'd start chemo. We'd see how he reacted. He was strong. He had a lot of life left to enjoy.

He qualified for a drug trial. The resident told us the trial could very well get him to the two-year mark. She said if we reached two years, he'd be close to a typical lifespan for a Shepherd. She meant to be reassuring, I know, but it made me furious.

He's not old. He's not done yet.

Neither John nor I wanted to sacrifice time with Lucas, but we were unwilling to sacrifice his quality of life. Driving home from Purdue, we decided that whether he had those few weeks or those two years, it would be the time of his life.

A week and a day later, his leg was gone.

Limp to amputation: three weeks.

Lucas stayed at the animal hospital for three days. They allowed us to visit once a day, and each time the vet techs regaled us with stories of his antics. "I thought we'd slowly walk out for a potty break," one said, "but he took off! He tried to run! I had to yell, 'Lucas, stop!' to get him to slow down."

Another told me she left him in one spot to step out for a second and came back to find him across the room pawing through medical supplies. True to form, Lucas wanted no part of a slow recovery.

The day before he came home, we rearranged our entire house. We knew we'd have to keep a close eye on him. John and I would sleep on the pullout sofa downstairs. I dragged our guest bedroom mattress downstairs and set it up alongside the sofa. Lucas would sleep there. I positioned the other couch and an armchair to create a barrier to keep him in one spot. I moved all my work materials downstairs so Lucas, Emmett, Cooper, and I would stay in that small hemmed-in-by-couches area during the day.

The first day he came home, I settled the dogs, set up my laptop, and started to work. After a few minutes, I climbed over the couch barrier and took the ten steps to the coffee pot. As I measured out scoops, I heard a shuffling from behind me. I turned around to see Lucas climbing up and over one of the other couches. "Lucas, no!"

A few days later, I took the boys out for a bathroom break—after the first three days, Lucas was entirely mobile without me having to hold the handle on his harness everywhere except stairs—and he started digging in the garden.

Two weeks of restriction felt like torture. He wanted to run. He wanted to jump. He wanted to play. Lucas wanted to be Lucas. He attempted escape at every turn. He dashed around the yard any chance he got. Even when he skidded out, or his legs slid out from underneath him, or he tripped and went down face-first, he popped back up and tried again.

Lucas's resilience during this time knew no bounds.

When the two weeks finally came to an end, we brought him back to the vet to have his stitches removed. Downy fur already grew over portions of the incision. He walked steadier. He fell less often. He wanted to *go*.

Thankfully, the vet said okay and off he went.

We started with slow walks down the block. I'd hold the handle on his harness while he hopped and bopped. The only time he struggled was going to the bathroom, but he conquered peeing quickly. It only took a few falls before he realized he could squat to go instead of lifting his leg.

Something we learned about three-legged dogs: Everyone wants to pet them.

John and I walked Lucas up and down the sidewalk in front of our house, slowly building up his strength. He could make it to the end of the block and back two times before he tuckered out. On our first pass, our next-door neighbors came out to say hi. We stood on the sidewalk chatting when someone from down the street walked straight for us. A stranger. Someone Lucas didn't know. I started to map our escape route.

As the guy approached, though, Lucas did the unthinkable.

He wagged his tail.

"A three-legged dog!" the guy exclaimed. "Can I say hi?"

Lucas approached him first, something John and I never thought we'd see. The man rubbed his head and patted his back.

"He seems steady on his feet," he said. Lucas's wound stood stark against his pale, fur-dotted skin. The guy looked at the incision. "How long has he been on three?"

"He just came off his exercise restriction," I said, "so a little more than two weeks. We're building up his strength going up and down the block."

Lucas wagged. He nosed the man to keep patting him. The man laughed and rubbed Lukey's head some more. "Have a good walk," he said as he continued on his way.

Later in the week, I took him to the vet for another check. I had some food and things to pass on to a friend who was going through a tough time, and he lived near the vet's office. "I'll meet you there," he said.

We met up early to catch up in the parking lot before Lukey's appointment. I figured I'd leave Lucas in the back of the car because Lucas meeting a strange man in a strange place?

No way.

As soon as we pulled up, I spotted my friend and parked next to his truck.

"Hi, big guy!" he said. Lucas wagged. I opened the door to let some air in for Lucas, and he became happy and wiggly, ready to meet a new friend. Before I could grab his leash, Lucas jumped down and ran straight toward my friend. Lucas asked for scratches and rubs while we chatted. We talked for a few minutes, then went into our appointment. In the lobby, Lucas greeted the staff and bopped around on his three legs. I couldn't believe this was my dog. My dog-reactive, stranger-danger, fearful, aggressive dog was…friendly?

After a few weeks of similar encounters, John and I started to joke that Lucas's aggression lived in that front leg of his. Once it was gone, so was his reactivity.

Meanwhile, we worked with Purdue to schedule him to start chemo.

By all reports, dogs tolerate chemo far better than humans, which is a huge relief. I knew how awful it was for me, but at least when I underwent chemo, I understood what was going on and why. I had the benefit of focusing on the light at the end of the tunnel. I couldn't explain cancer to Lucas. I couldn't convey to him: *Okay, this is going to suck for a while, but sick now, live longer.*

The protocol for his treatment was one dose of IV-administered carboplatin at Purdue every three weeks for four rounds. In the in-between weeks, he needed blood work at our local vet. The drug trial Lucas lucked into included an oral dose of piroxicam, an NSAID, every morning. I felt optimistic. His oncologist felt optimistic. His local vet did, too.

All the staging, ultrasounds, and X-rays were done before his first dose to see if there was observable metastasis. With osteosarcoma, the oncologists assume there is micrometastasis—a super small spreading of the cancer—because it's so aggressive and has almost always spread before the first symptoms appear. They also wanted to check his blood work to make sure he was healthy enough for chemo.

At his first dose, his platelets were low but not so low he had to skip treatment. So, on a sunny spring day, Lucas received his first round of chemo. Upon leaving Purdue, we were given two prescriptions to fill as needed: one for nausea and inappetence, and one for diarrhea.

That first round took it out of him. I drove Lucas home. He ate dinner and zonked. He slept all night—all of us curled around him on his mattress downstairs. In the morning, he woke up and puked. He struggled for a few days afterwards, and while his white counts were low, his energy and appetite recovered.

Three weeks later, I drove him back to Purdue for his next carboplatin infusion.

From our house to the vet school, the drive took two hours—each way. Lucas, never one for car rides, stuck it out because I promised him fast food burgers.

We arrived with time to spare. They checked him in and took him back.

When Emmett and Lucas visited Purdue, it turned into long days—four hours of driving aside—because the dogs were taken back and worked into student rotations. The schedule doesn't flow like it does at the vet's office because there isn't one vet and one tech doing everything. Instead, students work through rotations, which turns the day into a long one. I mapped out spots around West Lafayette where I could work: a Starbucks, a Barnes & Noble, the public library. I'd make my rounds of those spots, stop and eat lunch, then return to the animal hospital before discharge around four or five in the afternoon.

After I dropped Lucas off, I drove to Barnes & Noble with my work and a plan to purchase a fresh notebook to journal through all the stress. Unable to focus, my laptop and its empty screen perched on the table next to a quickly cooling coffee and an untouched scone. My mind whirled. I worried about Lucas in a way I never did with Emmett. With Em, I focused solely on the tests and the results. Captain Confidence, his gregarious nature allowed him to be friendly and comfortable everywhere, even at Purdue Oncology. That wasn't the case with Lucas. So, I worried. I worried he'd be scared. I worried he'd behave aggressively. I worried they wouldn't separate him enough from the other dogs. I worried and worried and worried, so much so that when my cell phone vibrated in my pocket, I startled so forcefully I almost fell out of my chair.

"We can't administer his chemo today," the resident said. "His counts are too low. You can come pick him up, and we'll reschedule for next week."

Nothing is ever safe.

I packed up my things and walked out to my car. I climbed in, shut the door, and dialed John on speakerphone.

I started to cry. "They won't give him his chemo!"

"What? Why?"

"His counts are too low. I have to pick him up and drive him back again next week and do this to him all over again."

John asked which counts were low and what they thought those low numbers meant. I didn't know. I hadn't asked any of those questions when she called. I was too tightly wound. I panicked, terrified something was really wrong, and didn't keep a clear head during the phone call.

When I arrived at the hospital, I took a few deep breaths and waited. They brought Lucas out, and he bopped over to me, wagging his tail and whining. I climbed out of my chair and sat on the floor so I could get my arms around him. He pushed his forehead against my chest. The tears welled up again. I wanted to bury my face in his fur and cry, but I needed to get it together to talk to his vet.

"We'll have him back next week," she said. "His counts should be back up, and we can do the next round."

"No," I said, my voice finally strong. "I can't go with a 'should' again. The drive is too hard on him. Can we have his counts checked locally, and if he's cleared, schedule chemo?"

She agreed and prepared the paperwork order for our local vet. We arranged to have his blood work done on Monday. If all was clear, I would drive him back to Purdue on Wednesday.

We climbed into the car. "I'm so sorry, Lucas," I said. "I'm so sorry to put you through this. We're doing it because we think it'll help. I'm so, so sorry." I drove him straight to McDonald's and ordered him a cheeseburger, then we started the long drive home.

Nothing is ever safe. But I've been through this.

We're resilient.

Resilience is another trait shared between us humans and our canines. Like people, dogs seem to show varying degrees of resilient behavior—some able to bounce back from trauma and abuse, while others are unable to recover.

How are dogs wired for resilience? What is it in their DNA that enables some of them to bounce back after being abused or abandoned? What about dogs makes them so able to change, especially when there are some humans perfectly capable of change who never even try or give an ounce of effort?

A 2019 paper posed these questions: "What are the key factors of psychological resilience in dogs? Why do some individuals recover swiftly from neglect, abuse or several years of harsh kennel environments, while some seem to be permanently traumatized by much milder adverse experiences?"

The authors concluded that resilience in dogs relies on a complex stew of genetic and environmental influences. These include good maternal care (did my dogs have *any* maternal care?), positive environmental enrichment, socialization, and breed. Plus, the authors noted the responsibility of the dog owner: a confident owner (gulp) could impact a dog's resilience, as could a secure attachment and positive interactions like playing and exercising together.

In other words, it's complicated.

When Lucas's counts recovered, we took him hiking. He loved tromping through the woods and digging up smells. He loved galloping through crunchy leaves and peeing on stuff. All summer, we took the boys to trails or parks every weekend. After our hike, we piled into the car and drove to a fast-food restaurant. Lucas tasted a cheeseburger from every fast-food restaurant in town. He even received a special delivery from a dear friend in California who shipped him an In-N-Out burger.

As the summer wore on, we regained hope.

He received his chemo, then came home and crashed. His numbers fluctuated after chemo visits, but he regained his strength in between doses and lived his life: walking, hiking, playing, though also a lot more sleeping.

A couple months into his treatment, John and I traveled to Maryland for John to serve as a groomsman in his friend's wedding. The first afternoon, before our bags were unpacked, my mother called. She and my dad stayed with the dogs and Newt when we traveled.

"Something's wrong with Lucas," she said.

My stomach hit the floor. My hands started to shake. This was my biggest fear when we left; I was terrified something would happen while we were gone. I took a deep breath and sat on the floor.

"What's going on?" I asked.

"He wanted to go outside. He's laying in the yard, and I keep calling him in, but he won't get up. He's just laying there. He's breathing, but he's not even lifting his head."

I exhaled. "Mom, go into the fridge and get the little bag of cocktail weenies out of the drawer. Shake the bag."

I heard rustling and rushing around, followed by the plastic crinkle as she shook the bag.

"Lucas, you little shit! You scared me half to death!" She picked up the phone. "I shook the bag and he popped right up."

"If he gets a warm patch of sun in the yard to himself, he never wants in," I said. "You can either leave him out there and he'll come in when he gets too hot, or shake the little bag of weenies."

When we arrived home from the trip, I learned my mom had decided to sleep downstairs on the couch with Lucas while my dad slept upstairs. They wanted to minimize his trips up and down the stairs. "I was so surprised when I woke up in the morning and there was Lucas on the chaise," he said. "He's not going to let three legs keep him from doing what he wants."

Lucas finished his final round of chemo. We celebrated with more takeout just for him. I told our vet I was concerned, though, because he kept dropping a small bit of weight at each check. With so much junk food each week, I figured he'd at least maintain his weight. She agreed it was concerning but suggested once the chemo effects wore off, he'd gain again.

We kept up with his hiking-and-chowing bucket list. In the process we discovered new trails, including a hidden gem off a side road where we never saw another person or pet. We rested. We cuddled. Lucas started to regain his energy but continued to experience long, tired bouts. He'd usually ask to go outside, then would lounge in the garden. One day, we all sat outside soaking up the sun. Lucas hopped over to his corner of the yard and started furiously digging up the flowers we'd just replanted—all with his one good front leg. We laughed and didn't bother to replant any of the garden.

Since the day I received my own diagnosis, cancer ruled my life.

I underwent four surgeries followed by a year of chemo followed by a decade of tests and checks and appointments and blood work. In the midst of my own cancer treatment, Emmett's diagnosis shifted everything. His surgeries. His chemo. His appointments, blood work, days at Purdue.

Next, came Lukey's diagnosis. Amputation. Chemo. Blood work. Radiology. We were either driving to Indy or West Lafayette every month. Every week found me in a doctor's office or a vet clinic. The busyness wore me out but also kept me from focusing on any one sadness, any one stress, for too long.

After my initial cancer staging, John started saying, "You were literally one millimeter from 'all we can do is keep her comfortable' versus being a candidate for chemo. A miracle."

Now, the only thing I had left was to hope for more miracles.

With Emmett, it was a statistical given that he only had three to six months left. With my diagnosis, 65 percent of patients didn't make it.

Emmett and I beat every odd stacked against us. I surpassed two years of being cancer free the same month Emmett surpassed a year and a half. Statistical anomalies, the both of us. I wished with my whole heart, my entire being, and every single scrap of my soul that everyone could be so lucky.

Lucas had a set of radiographs done in late summer and we celebrated their comparative clarity. Lucas moved slowly, though. He tired out more quickly and rested for longer stretches each day.

The chemo knocked him down, but we hoped to see him recover since his protocol was complete. Now we could move forward.

We scheduled repeat radiographs at Purdue for a couple months out and his biweekly blood work and X-rays at his regular vet. We drove home to figure out how to live this new normal.

When it was time for his chest X-rays a couple weeks later, I took him to our regular vet. Everyone at the practice greeted him with joy, and he bopped around, happy to see all his friends. The tech came and took him back. "Come on, Lucas! Follow me!"

And off he went like the good boy I knew was inside of him way back when I saw the first playful gleam in DC.

I sat on the bench and waited, unable to read my book or mindlessly scroll my phone. Instead, I sat. Took deep breaths. Focused on how far we'd come.

The exam room door opened, and when I looked up, Lucas's beloved vet stood in the doorway with tears on her cheeks. "I'm so sorry I'm crying," she said. She called me back.

Tumors riddled his lungs. The chemo didn't work. Metastatic osteosarcoma.

The tumors, they weren't small. They showed up within six weeks of completing his final round of chemo. One week they weren't there; two weeks later they were everywhere.

She presented me with three options: Do nothing but make him comfortable, drive him up to Purdue for weekly chemo IVs, or try an oral chemo at home. Neither chemo had been studied on his particular cancer, so effectiveness couldn't be known, nor could it be known whether one version is better than the other. We opted for the at-home version simply because we wanted to give him a fighting chance—versus doing nothing—but I couldn't make whatever time he had left a stressful round of drives and vet visits.

Even though the choice felt easy, the reality crushed me. On top of it all, he couldn't start either treatment until his white and platelet counts went back up. We felt it was the right choice to do the oral chemo, but before we left his appointment, we needed to make peace with the fact that he might not ever end up being a candidate if his white counts weren't high enough.

Somehow, through it all, I never thought we'd reach the end.

I took it as a given: Lucas would be fine. His treatment would work. He'd be another statistical anomaly like me and Em.

We had dangled by cancer's noose for five years at this point. Waiting. Watching. Panicking at every sign, symptom, and test. Me and Emmett dealt mentally and emotionally with each step in the process because we had time to process and move from stage to stage.

Emmett and I were given time.

This thing with Lucas? It swooped in and wrecked every mental and emotional defense we built over all these years of fighting. It snatched all the time he had left.

That's the thing about cancer: It's indiscriminate. It's unfair. It's cruel.

My own cancer still keeps me up at night—literally. Night sweats were a side effect of my treatment. During treatment, it felt like I'd never get a full night's sleep ever again; I'd wake up burning hot or freezing cold, drenched in sweat either way. The boys piled around me, but I couldn't sleep through the night. Now, I can't sleep through most nights because, it turns out, I hung onto the night sweats.

Sometimes, when I'm driving down the road or washing my hair or cleaning the floor, cancer fears pop into my head. *What if I die? I mean, obviously I'll die, but what if I die now, of this?*

And then, if I can rein it in, the fear is over. I look at Cooper or I look at my girls, and I know I need to stay grounded—not only for my own sanity, but to take care of my little herd. I remind myself when I'm going to my doctors' appointments and getting my scans: The rest is entirely out of my hands. I shake off my panic. Set it aside.

And then, when I can't rein it in, I cry big, hot, ugly tears. I lament how unfair it is. I don't want the fear of a recurrence over my head for the rest of my life, however long or short it may be. I panic because my daughters can't be left motherless and Cooper would never settle, never understand where I went. I worry about things like someone having to clean out my desk if I die, and what state is it in right now? Should I clean it up now, just in case? I'd hate for someone to be stuck with a disordered pile of random sticky notes and journals.

And then I feel sorry for myself. I ruminate and obsess and think through what it might be like for John to raise this whole family all on his own, and it follows me around like a black cloud until someone asks for a cup of juice or to turn on a show or to be let outside. I try to snap out of it, but it lingers sometimes. In those moments, I debate calling my dermatologist's office and asking for his home number, his pager, his email. I script the conversation in my head: "Look, I know I just had my appointment, and I know there's another one coming around in six months. However, I'd like to schedule another appointment for today if possible. And I want you to be extra thorough, extra cautious. Let's do this thing, because I'm having a mental breakdown about another round of melanoma, so I need you to do your thing and do it well and do it today so I can rest my brain."

But I don't. Or at least, I haven't yet.

And then the fear recedes, at least for a little while.

When John started his first new job outside of academia, one of the benefits was a spousal life insurance policy. So, of course, I filled out the paperwork to apply.

They rejected my application. Why? Because it's still statistically more likely I will die from cancer than not.

Truthfully, I've been doing okay with all this by simply putting one foot in front of the next, by focusing on one step and one action at a time. Keep moving forward. But that? That was a bummer.

I lost a lot of things to cancer, in addition to my life insurance policy qualifications: I lost hair. I lost weight (which I gained back double). I lost lymph nodes. I lost Lukey's golden years because we now knew cancer was going to take him too soon. *It's always too soon.*

I also lost the desire to pour my energy into things that aren't really my problem. I lost the self-absorption that allows negativity to seep in and leak out over day-to-day stuff. I lost the ability to tell the dogs "not now" when they shoved my fingers off the keyboard asking for a walk because, from now on, it will always and forever be, "Sure, let's go."

I've gained perspective on my priorities. I've always tried to be a positive person, but now I'm a grateful person, too. I'm naturally introverted, phone averse, and shy, but I've gained a bit of confidence that I hope has made me a better friend.

One clear evening, on the second of his twice-a-day meanders up and down our street, Lucas lost traction. He slipped. He wheezed. He stopped to catch his breath, then he laid down in the neighbor's backyard.

I continued to write about all this on my blog. I chronicled his condition, tests, treatments, and symptoms, all with the hope of helping someone facing a similar diagnosis with their beloved dog. One day I woke up to a comment accusing me of being too positive in my posts, that I needed to share the hard stuff, too.

It's all hard.

All of it. Every single second of loving these dogs we will surely outlive.

Every wag of his tail, every rest stop on a short around-the-block walk, every appointment, and every blood draw. It's all hard. But that's not what I want to focus on, ever. Focusing on the road ahead never allows us to live in the moment, the right now, the joy. That is how dogs live—in the moment, right now, with joy—and we would do well to emulate that.

The only way I ever want to move forward is by staying in this exact moment, a dog at my side, moving forward one little hop at a time.

CHAPTER 9

Dogs are Love, Plain and Simple

The day Lucas died, I taught my English course first thing in the morning. I stared out at the students' faces thinking just how incredible it was that not one person in that room knew I was about to lose one of my dearest friends. The inner lives of those around us teem with silent suffering, with thoughts and feelings we'll never know or understand. Life goes on outside, while inside someone's heart and soul are shattered shards of broken glass rattling around.

We knew it was coming. We knew, but still we hoped. When the oncologist showed us Lucas's lung X-rays and said, "I'm sorry," still, we hoped.

We noticed a bit of swelling in his back legs. He coughed a smidge. His best friend and our next-door-neighbor dog, Cady, stayed with us for the weekend, and the two rested together in the garden, side by side. Waiting. Then Cady went home and Lucas's legs were swollen more and his coughing became more pronounced, so we took him to our local vet to see if there was anything, anything at all we could do for him.

We hoped for something. We needed to hope.

"I'm so sorry," our veterinarian said.

She wrote her cell phone number on a slip of paper. She told us to call her, day or night, even on her days off, and she'd come over. We cried. She cried.

We took him home. We slept on the living room floor. We ordered him a pizza and a sub. We rubbed his ears and massaged his swollen legs. We told him we loved him over and over.

Some of his favorite people came by. They said "to visit," which we appreciated, but we knew. Everyone knew. He was saying his goodbyes. And even though he couldn't, he kept trying to jump up, to greet his friends with howls and wags and a spark in his big amber-brown eyes. They still shined with happiness those last few days, those final few hours. He had such a happy life.

Then the day came. He couldn't get up. No, it wasn't that he couldn't. He didn't want to try to get up. We knew it was coming, but it was such a shock. *Today is the day. How is it today?*

Lucas spent the morning basking in the sun in the backyard garden. His favorite place. He turned his face to the sun and took crumpled breaths. He knew, I think, as clearly as we did. It was his time.

I left him soaking up the sunshine with John, Emmett, and Cooper watching over him. I gave my class a project to do at home and dismissed them for the day. I drove home through a haze of tears. How can I be driving home to say goodbye to my special little guy? How can this be? How can I do this?

I texted his vet: It's today.

She texted back: I'll be there soon.

It was her day off.

John carried him in the house. We settled him onto a blanket in the middle of the living room floor. He rasped and laid down his head. He was tired. He was ready.

I'm not.

We sat with him. We hugged him and told him how much we loved him.

We let him go.

After he was gone, Cooper curled up against Lucas's stomach and nestled against him, just like he did as a puppy. It shattered us all, the tenderness of that gesture, the knowing.

Our vet and her tech left with Lucas's body—we were having him cremated. We were left with emptiness, the space Lucas had always filled: physically in his giant, bouncy, perma-puppy body, and emotionally, too, the years of worrying about him and for him.

Suddenly, the house felt oppressive. Like the emptiness would swallow us all whole. John scooped up the blanket and walked to the end of the alley to stuff it in the dumpster. Emmett and Cooper watched me pace the length of the kitchen island. Everything felt so quiet.

"Let's go for a hike," I said when John walked through the door.

We leashed up Em and Coop and drove to one of our favorite spots. The woods were quiet, too, but peacefully, not oppressively. We hiked the two-mile trail loop twice. Neither John nor I spoke. Emmett and Cooper plodded alongside. They felt Lukey's absence or could sense our distress, I could tell, because they stayed by our sides instead of exploring and sniffing.

Later, we returned home to a house that felt utterly empty.

That emptiness lingers, but it feels different now that time has passed. It's not about the habits or the routines or the daily Lucas-less-ness of our days. Instead, it's an ache for a presence that is somehow there, but not there.

Not a day goes by that we don't put him in the context of what's going on now. "Lucas would have loved this," or "Can you imagine if we had Lucas in this scenario?" We imagine he's still here, lurking around like a mischievous ghost-dog. We joke that he haunts Newt.

Each passing year, each milestone marker of more time without him, reminds me that it's been both forever and a blink, and I miss him.

His loss left a hole. That hole gapes. It's still there. It's changed shape a bit, the sides and edges are a little softer, a little lighter. Oh, but what I wouldn't give to bury my face in his thick, fuzzy neck and breathe him in.

The first few days after he died, I remember doing normal things, like standing in line at the grocery checkout or putting gas in my car. I looked around at all the people swirling past me and thought how amazing it was. Here I was, looking like a totally normal person doing totally normal things—swiping my card, getting my reusable shopping bags out of my purse—and all the people around me had absolutely no idea my world had crumbled only days ago.

I looked at the people ahead of me in line and wondered how many of them, how many people around us all the time, people who look totally normal doing normal-people things, have just had their worlds crumbled, too.

Amidst the loss, I felt—and still feel—astonished at my luck that I was the one to take care of Lucas in the first place, that he was my special little guy for eight wonderful, difficult, funny, frustrating years. He struggled and overcame so much, while staying true to himself. My life is richer forever because I got to bear witness to his evolution. I evolved right alongside him.

He left me with a life filled with deeper love and patience and gratitude and kindness. He was so special and fought so hard. He taught me about bravery and about joy, and his life—and, it turns out, his death—serves as a reminder to extend compassion whenever possible.

That's his legacy, and it fits him so well. I'll miss him forever, but I carry him with me. So, it'll be okay. But, of all the things that could've killed Lucas—his myriad, dangerous freedom runs, his fights with other dogs, getting kicked by a horse—it makes me sad and it makes me angry he succumbed to cancer. Especially because he never got the chance to be an old dog.

I really would've liked to know Lucas as an old dog.

When a dog dies, the physical space a dog filled while living—the bed by the fireplace, the worn circle of carpet under your desk, the harness on the hook by the door—becomes an echo.

When a dog dies, some people say, "Go get another. It'll help you get over it." Like it's possible to swap one dog for another. Some people say, "That's too bad. He was a good dog." Other people, my people, send love and lift you up, but say little because there are no words. At least, not any that make sense.

When a dog dies, the world moves on from the loss that cracked you open and split your heart because, yes, your dog was a good dog, and, yes, you'll get another someday, but *this dog, my dog* is gone. His echo fills so much space.

When a dog dies the world contracts because there's nothing that will ever recreate or replace that specific bond, that specific relationship. Of course you'll love other dogs and develop wonderful, strong relationships with other dogs, but this relationship, this friendship dies with your dog.

While we battled his cancer, I couldn't imagine a world without Lucas. His space, his presence, his personality—I realized it was all gone. Snuffed out too soon.

I also realized I have a lot of him that will never leave me.

I have the tactile memory of my hand in his fur. My fingers would weave deep into the thick, yellow coat. Tufts of it came out in clumps and drifted across our wood floors. Some of it, I'm sure, is still here, floating along underneath the baseboards or behind the fridge. One hunk of his hair was accidentally painted into our kitchen cabinets. I left it.

I have the muscle memory of my right arm holding his leash: He walked so nicely alongside me until a dog or a stranger went past. Then, he lunged to the far extent, straining my shoulder and back muscles until we reached safety. My shoulders still remember the ache of a difficult walk.

I have the emotional memory of the many hours we spent in various animal hospitals as he waged his battle against cancer.

I have the pride and humor and love and tenaciousness he brought to everything he did, including overcoming deep-rooted fears and phobias to become a gentle giant.

I have all that, and I have my memories. I have pictures and videos I can't bring myself to watch.

But what I don't have is him.

When a dog dies, it changes everything: the landscape, the color, your heart, the tapestry of your family.

Chances are, when your grandmother dies, you grieve but the impact on your actual day-to-day life is minimal. Unless you served as her primary caretaker, the sadness is about missing the person, but your daily life continues on as always.

When a dog dies, a moment happens—a coworker invites you to happy hour after work or a Saturday trip to the farmers' market runs really long—and you realize you don't have anyone waiting for you at home, waiting for you to let them outside, to pour a cup of kibble into a bowl. Toys aren't strewn around the floor. The dog bed in the corner of the kitchen gets tucked away, leaving a gaping space behind. The water dishes are picked up, washed, and stored in a closet. Same with the pile of leashes.

When a dog dies, it isn't just the loss of a friend. It's the loss of routine, of predictability. It's the loss of making decisions based around another's wellbeing. It's the loss of shifting in bed to accommodate another. It's the loss of setting down the yogurt container for your dog to lick out before it goes in recycling. It's the loss of the bark you expect every time the doorbell rings.

Grief is a strange thing. Well, it's not a thing. Or a person. Or a pet.

After Lucas died, I imagined grief as a place. It's a big, cavernous place with lots of rooms and hidden corners. Some are peaceful and calm. Others are dark and clawing.

Once you lose someone who matters, you move into this place, and the thing no one ever tells you, the thing no one ever talks about, is that you live here for the rest of your life. The loss never leaves you, so you can't leave the place.

Some spaces are calm. Peaceful even. Full of love and hope and joy and meaning. Then you pass a hallway and enter a different space, a hopeless one, a deep, echoing chamber with more darkness than light. But you keep going, and eventually you come back into the light. And this lasts forever, traveling through this place. Once you enter it, you're always there. And no one ever, ever tells you that.

The challenge with grieving for an animal is that it isn't respected or acknowledged, at least not in the way a human loss is. You're expected to move on. To find another pet. To stop crying. It was just a dog, after all.

Decades ago, research published in the scientific journal *Evolution and Human Behavior* found that, for most dog owners, the grief they experienced with the loss of their pet compared to the grief felt with the loss of a human loved one. And, even then, that wasn't new information in the scientific community. Researchers have found the same conclusion over and over: People grieve deeply for their dogs.

Yet, our culture doesn't honor that, not really.

In *Rising Strong*, Brené Brown wrote, "As individuals, we're afraid of the darkness grief brings. As a society, we have pathologized it and turned it into something to cure or get over. Owning our stories of heartbreak is a tremendous challenge when we live in a culture that tells us to deny our grief."

Even Dr. Brown is referring specifically to humans. I would add, it's even less acceptable on the whole when our grief is for an animal.

No one wants to see grief. No one wants to talk about it. At least not after a certain "acceptable" point. Plus, all that grief talk is aimed at people mourning other people. There's no wiggle room in that journey for pet loss. Practically the next day you'll hear: "So, when are you going to get another dog?"

Brown goes on to write about the longing stage of grief, when it's perfectly natural to engage in "magical or unrealistic thinking" and to wish fervently to "simply touch what we've lost."

Lucas filled such a specific spot in our lives and our hearts. It's a spot that can never again be filled, which makes its emptiness weigh all the heavier. Every time I feel like I have a handle on it, the emptiness gains ten, twenty, thirty pounds, and I drop it again.

Psychologist Julie Axelrod wrote about the significance of losing a dog: "Our pets provide us with emotional responses that are uninhibited by concern for how their expression appears to others. Many of our human relationships aren't that simple; they can be riddled with anxiety about rejection and other fears that often dictate how we behave and what we share. Our pets do not judge insecurity or imperfection. They are all-accepting in ways few humans can achieve." She went on to write about how pet ownership is like parenting, and the loss of a pet can disrupt a life filled with routines centered around caring for that pet.

Those routines, those places, feel impossible to fill. Where his water dish sat on the kitchen floor. Where the blanket bunched at the foot of the bed as he snoozed the day away. Where the toys scattered across the living room floor and annoyed me so much, but now I'd give anything to have his specific mess again because it would mean he was here.

The silence of the room when no one barks at the doorbell. Even harder to shake: the automatic cringe when the doorbell rings while your body awaits the barking that never comes.

If grief is a place, those are the echoes of the immediate loss. They resound and they reverberate, and eventually they wane. The blanket gets washed, folded, and stored. The dish and the toys get donated to the animal shelter. You stand up and answer the doorbell.

But what about Cooper and Emmett? What about Newt?

Did they suddenly feel like a puzzle with a missing piece? Did they even notice that a piece was ripped from them? Did they feel the heaviness of this loss like I did—or even at all? Did they notice Lucas was gone? Did they feel sad at all?

Do animals experience grief?

Before researchers dug into the question, a mountain of anecdotal evidence from various species from all parts of the globe indicated that, yes, animals grieve.

Elephants, for instance, are famous for their grief. They approach the bones of their deceased throughout all stages of decay. The elephants show agitation. They become subdued. Near the body, the elephants display increased social interaction. Can they be comforting each other?

Chimpanzees have been noted to show grieving-like behavior. Some, after experiencing a death, refuse to eat. In the case of a great loss, some chimpanzees have even starved to death. Some, like a mother who has lost her infant, refuse to set down the deceased body. Dolphin mothers do that, too, holding their dead calves at the surface of the water.

Among dogs, Hollywood immortalized Hachikō, the Akita who waited for ten years at the train station for his owner—who died at work, so he never made the return journey home. Since Hachikō's long wait, other dogs have captured attention with the same behavior, often being named in homage: the "Siberian Hachikō" or the "Ecuadorian Hachikō."

Does a prolonged wait—usually in vain—demonstrate grief?

It's possible that dogs simply don't understand the finality of death. Perhaps they wait and wait and wait because—ever the loyal, loving, optimists—they *know* their owner is coming back. Will arrive home. Will throw the ball once more. Or maybe dogs wait for their owners because, thrust into sudden aloneness, they don't know what else to do. We've bred a certain helplessness into our dogs, then we train them to be obedient.

Sure, most scientists argue that they can observe a behavior and make inferences from that behavior, but never really know or understand the motivation behind the behavior. But bioethicist Jessica Pierce writes, "The question is not 'Do animals grieve?' but 'How do animals grieve?'"

When I witnessed Cooper curled up against Lucas's body moments after he died, I knew Cooper felt something akin to my own sadness. I don't think he could possibly understand the permanence of death. He doesn't grasp time: a trip to the mailbox results in a homecoming celebration as big as a week away for work travel. Something, though, tipped him off. A smell? The sudden stillness to Lucas? Cooper knew something. He knew Lucas was gone.

Emmett seemed unfazed. He spent the entire time rooting through the veterinary technician's purse, searching for dog treats. "Emmett," she admonished him. "Show some respect."

Generally, Cooper was always a more thoughtful dog than Emmett. Emmett seemed to float through life on charm and good looks, while Cooper buzzed with anxiety. Cooper's river ran deeper than Emmett's, so it made sense to me that he grasped Lucas's loss more fully than Emmett did. Plus, Emmett knew a life before the other animals; Cooper did not.

Was Cooper sad? Yes.

Was Emmett? I'm not sure.

But emotions aren't necessarily quantifiable, and they exist on an unknowable sliding scale. My deepest grief may only scratch the surface of yours, while your anxiety might be a mere blip on my stress radar.

What is the scale for feeling sad about the loss of a pet? Since feelings are not measurable in the same way as hormones like oxytocin or dopamine, understanding human emotion requires finding ways to quantify subjectivity. This is a tough task for humans. It becomes impossible to quantify the emotions of our non-human friends, especially since we can't know for certain what or how an animal experiences emotions.

Even if we don't know what an animal's emotional experience is like, as it turns out, people are pretty darn good at understanding their dog's emotional state. Studies have shown that dog owners interpret their pet's behavior reliably and accurately, and not solely from an anthropomorphic lens based on assumptions. We don't simply ascribe characteristics to our dogs from our own human experience; we understand how they really are feeling. Research has shown that our assessment of our animal's emotions is accurate when the actual physical and physiological measures of stress are taken.

We know our dogs.

I knew, deep down, when the initial pain of the loss began to fade, the reality of creating a new identity would set in. We were no longer a family with three dogs and a cat. Lucas dying changed everything: our walk schedule, how we fed everyone, the dynamic between the animals, the stress level in the house. We were recreating our identities. Did the animals feel that, too?

There are days when the darkness descends. A shadow, almost invisible but heavy as iron, follows me. I enter an unlit room in my grief space. I wander around, dazed, as I make Violet a peanut butter and jelly sandwich or pour a glass of milk for Astrid. I wonder how these normal things go on after such profound losses, but they do. Life always moves forward, and eventually I stumble back into a well-lit space.

My light right now, the joy that brightens the dark corners: ghost Lucas messes with his artwork in our home. We have two portraits of him, one of which always falls crooked. It's on a wire hung with a level, but every so often it tilts on its axis. The other portrait? One day we noticed a huge slobber mark across it that we can't explain. So, he's here. I'm here.

This must be the place, the Lucas wing of my grief.

This part is flooded with memories.

Unbidden, I remember letting Emmett, Lucas, and Cooper out of the house, through the garage and into the backyard. The instant I pushed the outer door open, Lucas shot off at an angle.

I tore after him—Lucas dashing off was never a good thing—and took a second to take in the picture. An opossum was scrambling along the top of our fence, slipping and scratching and hissing, with Lucas on his back feet leaping at the terrified animal.

In the corner of that backyard stood a tree that grew into the fence. The tree twined around the fence and the fence was embedded into a piece of the trunk. Why wouldn't the owners have trained the tree in the opposite direction? Or moved the fence out? They didn't, and the result was a natural foothold for a single-minded dog scrambling after an opossum.

A flash of white hot panic engulfed me when I saw Lucas plant his back feet into that foothold, prepared to launch his entire body up and over the fence after the retreating opossum. I felt the tension in his muscles as I grabbed his back thighs and pulled as hard as I possibly could. It turned into a tug-of-war: He got his paws on top of the fence and pulled up with all he had, while I grabbed his hind legs and pulled down with all I had. Thankfully his angle was awkward and his purchase on the tree was weak. I won. We tumbled backward into the yard.

"Lucas! You idiot! You could've gotten hurt! Or lost!"

I marched everyone back into the house and let the adrenaline crash out of my body. Later that night, I cuddled him on my lap and apologized. I explained to him that I worried about him, if he got lost or hit by a car or encountered another dog or or or or—

"Lucas, I'm sorry. I love you."

A dog I spot on the grooming table of our local pet supply shop triggers another memory. Suddenly, I remember the girl with the Collie. Her name was CeCe. The Collie, not the girl. I never knew the girl's name.

I still hold the visceral memory of the icy cold that flooded my gut each time I saw them walking. She, the girl, let CeCe roam to the full extent of her flexible leash. Once the dog was out as far as she could go, the girl would stop walking, pull out her phone, and start scrolling while CeCe hung out within the perimeter of the flexi. Without fail, CeCe huffed and stared straight into the eyes of passing dogs. She didn't move at all. She stood stock still and stared. The rudest of rude dog behaviors, of course, but CeCe's person held the end of the flexi, completely oblivious as she tapped away on her phone. Lucas went bananas.

On our daily walks, I avoided them at all costs, scanning the horizon and checking down the path before turning. But one day they came around a corner and took me off guard. Lucas went bonkers. He launched himself forward, snarling as he pulled, scrabbled, clawed, and growled at CeCe. He pulled me right to the curb, almost into the street. Meanwhile, CeCe inched forward on her flexible leash and into the middle of the road and into the street. As her person stood on the sidewalk, face buried in her phone.

I pulled Lucas as hard as I possibly could to get away, but he was lunging with his full eighty pounds in the opposite direction. It was a battle. A woman pulled her car up and yelled, "Do you need help?"

I yelled back, "I just need that person to walk away!" She, CeCe's person, snapped her head up. She looked shocked. She glared at me and started walking…in the direction I was headed. Thankfully the car woman waited until CeCe passed us by, and we walked the other way. Lucas got a longer walk to circle around back home, and my heart got an additional jolt of adrenaline.

I pass a woman who smells distinctly of Chanel perfume, and I remember our neighbor, Hugh. An extremely tall, extremely thin man who lived down the hall from us in our DC condo. He owned a tiny little dog who Lucas hated. We were scratching the surface at rehabbing Lucas at that point, and that little dog set him off more than any other in our building. But Hugh didn't quite understand our situation with Lucas.

Whenever our paths crossed, Hugh leaned forward and rubbed Lucas's forehead. "Here, Lucas," he'd coo. "Let's get those wrinkles out of your face and then you can calm down." We were baffled by the thought that if Lukey's face didn't have those wrinkle lines he'd feel better, but Hugh was so sure of it. Of course, I remember he also sprayed his dog with expensive Chanel perfume. I didn't trust his dog sense because he purposefully masked his dog's innate smell, which probably added to Lukey's confusion and ire.

I remember the first dream Lucas appeared in after he passed away. In the dream, he ran far ahead of me along a cliff. He clearly enjoyed the freedom run, something he didn't get to do often enough in life. His ears flew behind him and his tongue flapped in the wind.

I remember the sudden realization that the cliff dropped off into a vast body of water. In life, Lucas could not swim. Some people say all dogs can swim, but Lucas truly could not. My hands started to shake, and I felt myself start to panic. *He's going to run off the edge. He'll fall in the water. He can't swim!*

I remember trying to yell, to call out, to shout his name, to stop him, to call him back to me. To please come back to me. But I couldn't speak. No sound came out. But, in the dream, I somehow heard him.

Don't worry. I can fly.

Off the edge of the cliff he went. He plummeted toward the water and at the final second, he flew. His body lifted up and he soared.

I watched him fly away, right over the water he couldn't swim in. I watched until he was almost gone, and when I woke up, I felt an enormous sense of peace.

Yes, he was gone, and he just said goodbye.

Epilogue

"We are all just walking each other home."
—Ram Dass

In 2015, when our herd included Emmett, Lucas, Cooper, and Newt, we prepared to move from Bloomington to central Indiana. On the weekends, we brought the dogs up to the new house to clean, paint, and unpack boxes. We accidentally painted one long piece of Lucas's fur into a cabinet—and, knowing his time was short—we left it as the paint dried. Ten years later, it's still there.

Lucas died before we moved. In fact, we waited until he passed because we didn't want to upend his life with a new house, new veterinarians, and new routines. We let him die in peace in the home where he spent the majority of his life, then our family relocated.

Time passed.

Emmett lived until age fourteen or fifteen, and then his body gave out on him. It was a slow decline, so we had plenty of time to enjoy his final months and were at peace when we said goodbye.

Cooper died at thirteen. He suffered from Canine Cognitive Decline, which is sometimes called "doggy dementia." While Violet had been sad as a toddler about the losses of Otto and Taco Fish, this was the first great loss in her life. Astrid, too. Helping them navigate grief for the first time in their young lives added a layer of complexity to my own sadness.

John and I swore after Cooper died in November 2023 that we would not adopt another dog until the spring. We wanted to wait until it was warm enough to potty train, and we needed time to process our grief.

Life threw us a curveball when we met an adoptable deaf and partially-sighted dog named Penny. She jumped into Violet's lap and that was that. We adopted Penny in January 2024 only two short months after we lost Cooper.

Penny came to us from a hoarding rescue. She's a mix of Catahoula and pit bull—mostly white, except for her hind end, which is speckled with brown spots, some of them heart-shaped.

She is the sweetest, calmest, quirkiest little princess. She's gentle in all things, but she's also quite odd. She won't walk down the front hallway in our house. She won't step foot in the dining room or any of the bathrooms. She takes all her treats and buries them in the couch cushions instead of eating them.

Then, one year later, in January 2025, we adopted Stola, a pit bull rescue who is also deaf. So far Stola has chewed through two seatbelts in my van, the kitchen baseboards, a library book (*Onyx Storm*), three leashes, two dog beds, and untold numbers of Barbies and accessories. And Stola is continuing the work puppy Cooper started on the corner of the ottoman.

Thank goodness she's ridiculously cute.

I often wonder what lessons Penny and Stola will teach me over the course of their always-too-short lives.

The boys come up often, especially as we compare their antics to Penny's and Stola's. Violet and Astrid talk about Cooper in the present tense still, though they are both smitten with Penny and Stola.

Our home has a hallway dedicated to the portraits of Emmett, Lucas, and Cooper, and their framed pictures are scattered around the house. When you say goodbye, they're never really gone. They live on in our stories. And in a piece of fur painted into a kitchen cabinet.

References

American Heart Association. "To be a relentless force for a world of longer, healthier lives." (n.d.). *Www.Heart.Org*. https://web.archive.org/web/20151225174904/http://www.heart.org/HEARTORG/GettingHealthy/Owning-a-Pet-May-Protect-You-from-Heart-Disease_UCM_453586_Article.jsp

Archer, J. (1997). Why do people love their pets? *Evolution and Human Behavior, 18*(4), 237–259. https://doi.org/10.1016/s0162-3095(99)80001-4

Aschwanden, C. (2014, December 15). "Getting a dog? A pet might improve your health." *The Washington Post*. http://www.washingtonpost.com/national/health-science/getting-a-dog-a-pet-might-improve-your-health/2014/12/12/5e00cebe-7f27-11e4-9f38-95a187e4c1f7_story.html

Berns, G. (2017). *What It's Like to Be a Dog: And Other Adventures in Animal Neuroscience*. Basic Books.

Bibaud, Remy. (2020, February 25). "Grieving the Loss of a Pet By Julie Axelrod - Guest Blog." *Pet Perennials*. https://

petperennials.com/blogs/news/grieving-the-loss-of-a-pet-by-julie-axelrod-guest-blog

Blackwell, Emily J., Caroline Twells, Anne Seawright, and Rachel A. Casey. (2008). "The relationship between training methods and the occurrence of behavior problems, as reported by owners, in a population of domestic dogs." *Journal of Veterinary Behavior 3* (5): 207–17. https://doi.org/10.1016/j.jveb.2007.10.008

Briggs, B. H. (2017, July 18). "How did dogs become our best friends? New evidence." *BBC News*. https://www.bbc.com/news/science-environment-40638584

Brkljačić, Tihana, et al. "The Beginning, the End, and All the Happiness in Between: Pet Owners' Wellbeing from Pet Acquisition to Death." Anthrozoös 33.1 (2020): 71-87.

Brown, B. (2017). *Rising Strong: How the Ability to Reset Transforms the Way We Live, Love, Parent, and Lead.* Random House.

Brulliard, K. (2016, June 29). "We love stories about dogs mourning their owners. But they might not be what they appear." *Washington Post*. https://www.washingtonpost.com/news/animalia/wp/2016/06/29/we-love-stories-about-dogs-mourning-their-owners-but-they-might-not-be-what-they-appear/

"Can Dogs Smell Cancer?" (n.d.). *Roswell Park Comprehensive Cancer Center*. https://www.roswellpark.org/cancertalk/202008/can-dogs-smell-cancer#:~:text=In%20various%20experiments%2C%20dogs%20have,subjects%20with%20no%20known%20cancer

Callier, V. (2020, July 31). "What a Crowdsourced Study Taught Us About How Dogs Learn." *Smithsonian Magazine*.

https://www.smithsonianmag.com/science-nature/how-much-dogs-intelligence-hereditary-180975448/

Dogtime. (2009, May 30). A brief history of breeding. *DogTime.* https://dogtime.com/dog-health/general/915-breeding-history#:~:text=Breeding%20as%20we%20know%20it,herding%20dog%2C%20or%20lap%20dog

Davidson, A. P. (2023, February 23). The Breeding Soundness Examination in Dogs and Cats. *Merck Veterinary Manual.* https://www.merckvetmanual.com/management-and-nutrition/management-of-reproduction-dogs-and-cats/the-breeding-soundness-examination-in-dogs-and-cats

"Dogs' physical traits controlled by small number of genetic regions, researcher finds." (2010, August 11). *ScienceDaily.* https://www.sciencedaily.com/releases/2010/08/100810203503.htm

Evans-Wilday, Aislinn & Hall, Sophie & Hogue, Todd & Mills, Daniel. (2018). "Self-disclosure with Dogs: Dog Owners' and Non-dog Owners' Willingness to Disclose Emotional Topics." *Anthrozoös.* 31. 353-366. 10.1080/08927936.2018.1455467.

Evolution: Library: "Evolution of the Dog." (n.d.). https://www.pbs.org/wgbh/evolution/library/01/5/l_015_02.html

Goldman, R. (2021, October 14). "How to Cope When You're Grieving the Loss of a Pet." *Psych Central.* https://psychcentral.com/lib/grieving-the-loss-of-a-pet/

Granneman, J. (2019, November 7). "Cat Lover? You're More Likely to Be an Introvert." *Psychology Today.* https://www.psychologytoday.com/us/blog/the-secret-lives-introverts/201910/cat-lover-you-re-more-likely-be-introvert

Greenfieldboyce, N. (2016, August 30). "Their Masters' Voices: Dogs Understand Tone And Meaning Of Words." *NPR.* https://www.npr.org/sections/health-shots/2016/08/30/491935800/their-masters-voices-dogs-understand-tone-and-meaning-of-words

Grimm, D. (2015, April 16). "How Dogs Stole Our Hearts." *Science.org.* https://www.science.org/content/article/how-dogs-stole-our-hearts#:~:text=Mutual%20gazing%20had%20a%20profound,female%20owners%20a%20300%25%20increase.

Hare, B. & Woods, V. (2021). *Survival of the Friendliest: Understanding Our Origins and Rediscovering Our Common Humanity.* Random House.

Hecht, J. (2016, April 30). "The History of Science in Animal Shelters." *Scientific American Blog Network.* https://blogs.scientificamerican.com/dog-spies/the-history-of-science-in-animal-shelters/

Hecht, J., Miklósi, Á., & Gácsi, M. (2012). "Behavioral assessment and owner perceptions of behaviors associated with guilt in dogs." *Applied Animal Behaviour Science, 139*(1–2), 134–142. https://doi.org/10.1016/j.applanim.2012.02.015

Horowitz, A. (2011). "Theory of mind in dogs? Examining method and concept." *Learning & Behavior, 39*(4), 314–317. https://doi.org/10.3758/s13420-011-0041-7

Janssens, M., Eshuis, J., Peeters, S., Lataster, J., Reijnders, J., Enders-Slegers, M., & Jacobs, N. (2020). The Pet-Effect in Daily Life: An Experience Sampling Study on Emotional Wellbeing in Pet Owners. *Anthrozoos, 33*(4), 579–588. https://doi.org/10.1080/08927936.2020.1771061

Kis, A., Hernádi, A., Miklósi, B., Kanizsár, O., & Topál, J. (2017). "The Way Dogs (*Canis familiaris*) Look at Human Emotional Faces Is Modulated by Oxytocin. An Eye-Tracking Study." *Frontiers in Behavioral Neuroscience, 11*. https://doi.org/10.3389/fnbeh.2017.00210

Kluger, J. (2018, July 20). "Why Dogs and Humans Love Each Other More Than Anyone Else." *Time*. https://time.com/5342964/human-bond-dog-thoughts/

"Major Study Indicates That Therapy Dogs Provide Significant Benefits to Families of Children Undergoing Treatment for Cancer." (2017, December 22). *American Humane Society*. https://www.americanhumane.org/press-release/major-study-indicates-that-therapy-dogs-provide-significant-benefits-to-families-of-children-undergoing-treatment-for-cancer/

McAndrew, F. T. (n.d.). "Why losing a dog can be harder than losing a relative or friend." (2017, March 9). *The Conversation*. https://theconversation.com/why-losing-a-dog-can-be-harder-than-losing-a-relative-or-friend-68207

Miklósi, Á. (2009). "Evolutionary approach to communication between humans and dogs." *Veterinary Research Communications, 33*(S1), 53–59. https://doi.org/10.1007/s11259-009-9248-x

Mueller, K. (2024, November 6). "Why Introverts and Pets Just Get Each Other." *IntrovertDear.Com*. https://introvertdear.com/news/introverts-pets-perfect/#:~:text=Many%20introverts%20are%20hardcore%20animal%20lovers%20(me!).&text=Because%20animals%20fulfill%20a%20very,we%20need%20as%20we%20recover.

Nagasawa, M., Mitsui, S., En, S., Ohtani, N., Ohta, M., Sakuma, Y., Onaka, T., Mogi, K., & Kikusui, T. (2015). "Oxytocin-gaze positive loop and the coevolution of human-dog bonds." *Science. 348*(6232), 333–336. https://doi.org/10.1126/science.1261022

Nature vs. Nurture: (Genes Vs. Environment). (2023, December 11). *MedicineNet.* https://www.medicinenet.com/nature_vs_nurture_theory_genes_or_environment/article.htm

Morell, V. (2020, February 20). "New sense discovered in dog noses: the ability to detect heat." *Science | AAAS.* https://www.sciencemag.org/news/2020/02/new-sense-discovered-dog-noses-ability-detect-heat

Patton, P. (n.d.). "Do Elephants Grieve Their Dead?" (2021, February 8). *A Moment of Science - Indiana Public Media.* https://indianapublicmedia.org/amomentofscience/do-elephants-grieve-their-dead.php

"Pet Statistics." (n.d.). *ASPCA.* https://www.aspca.org/helping-people-pets/shelter-intake-and-surrender/pet-statistics

Pierce, J. (2018, August 24). "What the grieving mother orca tells us about how animals experience death." *Lifeandnews.com.* https://www.lifeandnews.com/articles/what-the-grieving-mother-orca-tells-us-about-how-animals-experience-death/

Powell, L., Stefanovski, D., Siracusa, C., & Serpell, J. A. (2021). "Owner Personality, Owner-Dog Attachment, and Canine Demographics Influence Treatment Outcomes in Canine Behavioral Medicine Cases." *Frontiers in Veterinary Science, 7.* https://doi.org/10.3389/fvets.2020.630931

Quervel-Chaumette, M., Dale, R., Marshall-Pescini, S., & Range, F. (2015). "Familiarity affects other-regarding preferences in pet dogs." *Scientific Reports*, *5*(1). https://doi.org/10.1038/srep18102

Response to Threat. (n.d.). *ISpeakDog*. http://www.ispeakdog.org/response-to-threat.html

"Restorative Niches": Author Susan Cain on the Need for 'Quiet.'" *Knowledge at Wharton Podcast.* (2012, April 4). https://knowledge.wharton.upenn.edu/article/restorative-niches-author-susan-cain-on-the-need-for-quiet/

Robinson, L. & Segal, J. (n.d.). "The Health and Mood-Boosting Benefits of Pets." *HelpGuide.Org*. https://www.helpguide.org/articles/mental-health/mood-boosting-power-of-dogs.htm

Summerfield, J. (2016, July 8). "The Dark Side of Socialization: Fear Periods and Single Event Learning." *Dr. Jen's Dog Blog*. http://www.drjensdogblog.com/the-dark-side-of-socialization-fear-periods-and-single-event-learning/

Thelwell, E. M. (2019). Paws for Thought: A Controlled Study Investigating the Benefits of Interacting with a House-Trained Dog on University Students Mood and Anxiety. *Animals*, *9*(10), 846. https://doi.org/10.3390/ani9100846

Tiira, K. (2019, November 15). "Resilience In Dogs? Lessons From Other Species." *Veterinary Medicine : Research and Reports*. https://doi.org/10.2147/vmrr.s189566

Acknowledgments

It takes the time and effort of so many wonderful, kind-hearted, lovely people to bring a book to life. Truly, if I could thank each and every one of you who contributed to this in some way—going all the way back to elementary school and the first teacher who encouraged my writing—it would be another full-length book. Instead, I'll attempt to be brief, knowing I'll probably miss someone. (If it's you, my sincerest apologies.)

To the publishing pros who believed in this book and gave it a home: my dog-loving agent, Cole Lanahan, who is kind, supportive, and brilliant; my editor, Caitlyn Limbaugh, and copy editor, Rachel Paul, who worked to ensure this was the best book possible; and the countless behind-the-scenes editors and designers and marketers who contribute their expertise. Thank you all for your enthusiasm and generosity throughout the life of this project. Thank you, Bekah and Nikki at The Method Agency, for giving me a whole new set of skills and a fresh mindset about publishing, marketing, promotion, and social media. Thank you both for being supersmart, encouraging, and generous with your time and talent.

It's impossible for me to articulate how many people loved and supported me through the years of writing my blog and then this project. If I could wrap my arms around you all and give you a big squeeze right now, I totally would. I'd also like to scritch your dog. To my blogging besties, thank you for being you. Genuinely, you are shining examples of compassion, love, and authenticity, and I'm honored I still get to be friends with you after all these years. To my DWAA and CWA friends, you, too, champion the love of animals and journalistic integrity.

Thank you to my critique group—Lisa Fabish, Heidi Colonna, Diane Herbert, and Chrissy Holm—whose insights made this book better, and your friendship kept me motivated when it got difficult. I miss seeing your faces on Zoom each month, and I can't wait to keep reading all your wonderful books!

And then there are the people who believe in the power of pets, the people who don't think I'm a loon when I need to talk through the most minute details of dog (and cat!) behavior. Thank you for being such a champion of dogs and dog writing. Carol, Erik, Sof, Tracey, Deb, Katherine, this list could go on forever: You've all impacted me and my pets by sharing your love, compassion, generosity, and friendship.

Throughout my life, I've been lucky to be surrounded by people who I honestly can't believe are still my friends considering I rarely text back, don't answer my phone, and will pretty much only meet up if it's not crowded and there will be parking. Je'ree, what would I do without you? Erin, thank you for loving my girls so well and always, always asking how my book is coming along. Ann Wesley, it's been a long while, but thank you for loving my boys and for being a positive force for good in our lives during a difficult season.

Dear Jodi, you said I couldn't dedicate this book to you, but it's to you in secret. I'm lost without you, so I'll see you on Sunday, okay?

None of this would be possible without my wonderful parents who have never called me nuts for pursuing this made-up career. They support and cheerlead me every step of the way, and I can't even begin to share my gratitude for your unshakable belief in me.

John, thank you for the bottomless love and patience and hyping up and coffee and hugs and advice and championing. You read every word I write before it's been edited and make me and my writing better by loving me so completely. Violet and Astrid, I'd need an entire book to thank you for being the wonderful, bright sparks that light up my day. I'm honestly not sure what I did to deserve such remarkable children.

None of this would be possible without Emmett, Lucas, Cooper, and now Penny, but hopefully the entire book comes close enough to thanking them for the impact they've had on my life and the lives of all the people they've touched over the years.

Thank you to the OMD community, the group of people who have shared their dogs with me for the past fifteen years, who have shared laughter and tears over the stories in these pages, and who have kept me going during the most difficult moments of my life. We are all connected through this mutual love of our dogs, and I am grateful and touched that you've welcomed my words into your life.

Finally, to the teachers and librarians who keep books on shelves and in hands: Thank you for fighting the good fight.

About the Author

Photography by Austyn, Carmel, Indiana.

Maggie Marton writes about dogs and cats from her home outside Indianapolis. She's the blogger behind *Oh My Dog!* (ohmydogblog.com), which has appeared in *The New York Times*, *Animal Wellness Magazine*, and *Dog Fancy*. She studied anthropology at Butler University and earned her master's in writing from Johns Hopkins University.

Maggie's work has received numerous awards from the Cat Writers' Association, the Dog Writers Association of America, DogTime Media, Fear Free Pets, and the American Association of Feline Practitioners.

Active in animal welfare and rescue, Maggie served on a nonprofit Board of Directors, worked with pit bull education and advocacy organizations, and appeared in the renowned

Pinups for Pitbulls calendar and book with her late therapy dog, Emmett.

She shares her house with a deaf and partially-sighted rescue pup named Penny, cats Ripley and Newt, half a dozen fish tanks, two daughters, and a very patient husband.